The Spirit of Excellence

RESTAURANTS, CHEFS, RECIPES AND COGNACS

Bon ViVant Publishing Inc
1601 West MacArthur Boulevard Suite 6G
South Coast Metro Ca 92704 USA

Copyright © 2002 by David Shaw
Rémy Amerique Inc and Bon ViVant Publishing Inc
Photographs copyright © Bob Hodson Photography, ©Matt Israel

Designed by Donald Kase
Production by Gary Morris

Printed In Great Britain
0-9722750-0-2
Library of Congress cataloguing- in- Publication data
Bon ViVant Publishing, Inc.

The Spirit of Excellence –
RESTAURANTS, CHEFS, RECIPES AND COGNACS
(Volume 1)

David Shaw, International First Impressions,
Bon ViVant Publishing Inc and Rémy Amerique Inc

ISBN 0-9722750-0-2

Introduction

BY DAVID SHAW (PUBLISHER INTERNATIONAL FIRST IMPRESSIONS MAGAZINE)

I have always believed that a guidebook should offer three crucial ingredients: information, entertainment and education. The last point in particular is also true, regarding the theme of this book. Rémy Martin of Cognac, France, have been an innovator in the education of the palate and in the art of fine cognac making. Now with one of the greatest brigades of chefs ever assembled under one cover, together with their extraordinary cognac-savant, Vincente Géré, they are proud to pair their classic blends, with the wonderful gastronomic delights from the hands of these creative geniuses.

The result is *"The Spirit of Excellence"* – a definitive guide covering 30 of the USA's greatest restaurants, their executive master chefs and some of the most celebrated signature recipes in the world.

I should also record my indebtedness to Rémy Amerique for their insight, support and above all, belief in my longstanding ambition to publish this unique guide offering you, the reader, a chance to travel, experience and enjoy throughout these pages.

Napoleon Bonaparte famously remarked *"An army marches on its stomach".*

This is also a tribute to many of the chefs presented here. Some, not natural-born Americans, worked their way around the kitchens of their homelands (as did many of the young people working in the Windows on the World on the 107th floor of One WTC) and then came to America to be free and realize their own American dream. In the aftermath of September 11th, 2001, and without any prompting or appeal, many of the chefs and restaurants found in these pages, opened their hearts to provide round the clock sustenance to feed our universal heroes at "Ground Zero". That food sustained so many to keep the flag of rescue flying against the most daunting of odds.

We Salute you!

Finally, to many readers, for the first time, here is an opportunity to experiment with a fine cognac served to complement an exceptional meal in the dining room of a great culinary icon. This book is different, it is creative but above all, it most certainly will enhance our appreciation for food and our continuing evolution in good taste.

-And all in the Spirit of true Excellence.

Taste, learn, enjoy.

With sincere good wishes,

David Shaw
Publisher- International First Impressions of Dining

DAVID SHAW

Contents

THE SPIRIT OF EXCELLENCE

*An Epicurean odyssey in the true
Spirit of Excellence*

Please note, that in some cases, restaurant details and menu items may have changed since press date. However, we would like to reassure our readers, that the utmost accuracy has been diligently maintained wherever and whenever possible in the compilation of this book.

Foreword

BY VINCENT GÉRÉ   MAÎTRE DÉGUSTATEUR DE RÉMY MARTIN

For as long as I can remember, I have always enjoyed the best bottles at the table. I have a clear memory of my childhood, growing up between Cognac and Bordeaux, with my father, a winemaker and cognac maker, asking me what I thought of this or that rare sample from a winery, distillery or other cellar. Generally these tastings took place over dessert or cheese at the end of a Sunday lunch.

Naturally, when I became a winemaker myself, I continued to match wines, champagnes, sherries and cognacs from the Fine Champagne area with food. I remember challenging sessions with Daniel Thibault, the Chef de Cave of Charles Heidsieck Champagne, seeking to find a precise match for his latest 'babies' with selected bouchées, tasting-sized portions of a variety of dishes.

During my years as Head Winemaker at the Blue Pyrenees Estate in Australia, it even got to the point where I was working on my blends of Australian wines during lunch, seeing how they reacted and getting to know them better. Over thirty trips to China setting up wineries there for Rémy Martin, I discovered the culture of celebrating with cognacs drunk throughout banquets where there were up to fifteen dishes and their complex spices to play with.

As I became more and more involved in the making of Rémy Martin cognacs, it quickly became obvious to me how lucky I was to be experiencing the ultimate concentration of wine flavors. The eaux-de-vie are from the best vineyards, the distillation on the lees concentrates their textures, and the richness from the long ageing in barrels corresponds to a maturation level rarely seen in wines.

I entered the territory of perfume you can drink: Top notes, aromatic heart, base notes, first sip, mouth-feel, balance of the finish, length – twenty, fifty, a hundred flavors at a time; two hundred, three hundred, seven hundred cognacs present in one assemblage, ten times the complexity of great wines. Working on the blends is a challenge for your taste, for all your points of reference. Here in Cognac, we are bathed in French culture and memories. A very different cultural experience compared to a tasting during a Chinese banquet in Shanghai!

We started working on matching food and cognacs with French chefs, in the Cognac region at first. The 'Only Rémy' Dinners were born. The restaurant kitchens became real taste laboratories as the chefs discovered the varied possibilities in pairing food with our cognacs. Their understanding changed, as did ours, it was almost as if they were re-inventing our cognacs for us.

When I met David Shaw, I discovered someone with the same natural belief in food and drink as important cultural experiences. He saw the differences this way of looking at things can create. From this point, we embarked on the biggest of adventures, travelling throughout the United States. Our goal was simple, if ambitious: to work with the greatest chefs, all important personalities of achievements, passion and with a genuine need to experiment with flavors. In other words, to unleash TASTE.

So the adventure consists of pairing our cognacs with the best signature dishes from some of the best chefs in the United States. This selective focus reveals spectacular facets of our cognacs because each dish brings out different and unique aspects. Further on in the book, I have explained the fundamentals of tasting and pairing, how to look for matches, synergies, fusions. Give each pairing the luxury of time: it is a price worth paying to savor rare aromas, huge flavors, delicate textures on the palate, balanced finish, layers of finesse, incredible length.

I trust that apart from enjoying the food served at the restaurants featured in this book, the recipes will make you want to rush down to your local deli or wine merchant before cooking and opening one or more of the cognacs in the Rémy Martin range. V.S.O.P; 1738 Accord Royal; X.O Excellence; Extra; Louis XIII : now you can TASTE them, fired with enthusiasm and confidence... the choice is yours!

Thank you to these great American Chefs for allowing all of us at Rémy Martin to fall in love all over again with our very special spirits.

Vincent Géré

Vincent Géré
Maître Dégustateur de Rémy Martin

" I love this book because it is a celebration of food and cognac which fires the imagination. As it explores, explains and pays homage, it is as close to perfection as an introduction to great cognacs is ever likely to be for the beginner. The cognac connoisseur can also learn from it. This is a new book exploring a very old subject, a modern taste of an ancient spirit. Here are the ultimate tastings in dishes and pairings which give you the feeling that you can smell, savor, enjoy, and learn at the same time. The aim is to take you inside the glass, to immerse you in the atmosphere of the restaurants and our cellars: to make the cognac live for you. We feel that understanding cognac will help you enjoy it more. What I call becoming 'cognac intelligent'."

VINCENT GÉRÉ

A History of Cognac

- AS A PRODUCT, A COUNTRY AND A WAY OF LIFE

"It is said that everyone knows two words of French and one of them is Cognac. It is a place of spirit and the spirit of a place. Both are very special."

Cognac the place is a town of quiet charm in western France, north of Bordeaux. Its medieval heart lies on the Charente River ('*the prettiest stream in all my kingdom*', said Henri IV four hundred years ago) which winds its placid way through the area entitled to make the spirit that is Cognac. The landscape is gentle and clothed with over a quarter of a million acres of vineyards.

All cognacs are brandies but not all brandies are cognacs...

There have been vines on this land since Roman times, but Cognac, as we know it, dates from the last half of the seven-

teenth century when, for reasons not entirely certain but probably to do with taxes and economics of transport, the *Cognaçais* switched from shipping their wine to distilling it into the spirit first called brandewijn by the Dutch and 'burnt wine' by the English, its two main export markets. So brandy was born: the only spirit – as it still is today – to be distilled from grapes rather than grain.

At first, brandy was most popular with the military for its medicinal properties. Both the British and Dutch navies used it to 'sterilize' the impure water their ships carried at sea while both navies and armies recognized its antiseptic quali-ties on wounds and 'anaes-thetic' abilities (when drunk

in large quantities) if musket balls had to be removed or limbs amputated. It is probably safe to say that this brandy had neither the taste nor complexity of cognac today.

By the nine-teenth century the Cognac area was the largest grape-growing region in the world although its wines were almost all distilled. As quality improved and

brandies started to be named according to the region they came from, they were further defined by area and quality. *Champagne de Cognac* (referring to the region just below Cognac the town) was considered superior to brandy from the Bois (the wooded areas nearer the coast) and so commanded a higher price. This is still true today.

Given the French obsession with the quality of their food and wine, it was only to be expected that quality controls would eventually apply to Cognac. In 1909 a decree of the French government specified the geographic area of Cognac and marked it out into six regions, or *crus*.

From the twin centers, named Grande Champagne and Petite Champagne (the word *champagne* in French originally meant "open countryside" and here has nothing to do with bubbles), the other four – Borderies, Fins Bois, Bons Bois and Bois Ordinaires – spread out in roughly concentric rings towards the Atlantic coast.

Only brandies made within these borders could legally be called cognac, a decree reinforced in 1938, when each of the crus was awarded its own *Appellation d'Origine Contrôlée* (AOC). From then on also, only cognac made from Grande Champagne and Petite Champagne grapes (with at least half from the former) could be called Fine Champagne Cognac. The word 'fine' on its own on a cognac bottle is virtually meaningless.

The Rémy Martin Dynasty...

At the end of the seventeenth century, as brandy was entering adolescence, a young boy was tending the vines on his family's farm at Rouillac, about 15 miles from Cognac. His name was Rémy, the son of Denis and Marie Martin. He grew into an ambitious and clever young man who could see the future in distilling. He added more vineyards to the family property and by 1724, married and prosperous, he was ready to expand. The House of Rémy Martin, growers and merchants, was formed.

He was to be the only *Cognaçais* to create one of today's 'big four' cognac houses. (The other three were founded by merchants and foreigners: Richard Hennessy (in 1765) from Ireland; Jean Martell (in 1715) from Jersey, while Emmanuel Courvoisier (1835) was a Parisian – just as foreign in rural France!) Rémy Martin was also the only one to have his roots in the land. When he died at the age of seventy eight, in 1773, he left a thriving business to his grandson, another Rémy Martin.

Over the next two centuries, the firm of Rémy Martin continued to grow despite the political upheavals of the French Revolution, the loss of its main export markets during the Napoleonic wars, two world wars and German occupation. But for them as for everyone else in Cognac, the worst disaster of all came in the 1870s when *phylloxera*, a tiny aphid, struck. By 1880 the Cognac region was a desolate landscape of dead vines.

Growers and merchants were ruined in their hundreds. For years afterwards, 'phylloxera' was the threat hurled at naughty children.

But in some ways, *phylloxera* made Cognac the spirit it is today. It took more than ten years for the region to recover, and when it did it was thanks to a Texan, whose nursery at Denison on the Red River was found, in 1887, to have American rootstock (which was immune to the deadly insect) suitable for both the chalky Cognac soil and its white grape varieties.

Replanting was expensive and in some areas which had never produced very good wines it was not worthwhile. In that sense, overall quality was improved. The wholesale replanting of vineyards could also be done scientifically, and ordered rows, with room between for a horse-drawn plough, replaced the previous closely-grown, higgledy-piggledy vines. That, too, improved quality.

The Rémy Martin Centaur...
The Symbol of Taste

Fortunately, some *Cognaçais* combine several contradictory qualities which not only help them overcome disasters but also make the making of cognacs better. Cognac takes its time to distill and years to mature, so patience and farsightedness are needed. On the other hand, so is a shrewd head for business and a certain willingness to take risks. And when you are making something designed for export all over the world, to nations

speaking many languages, you also need an instinctive flair for marketing. You need a logo with a strong global identity that doesn't offend one or more nationalities.

As long ago as 1870, Rémy Martin's great-great-grandson, Emile Rémy Martin, was pondering the problem. He decided on a Centaur.

Like centaurs themselves, Emile Rémy Martin was a stargazer – a keen astronomer – and a Sagittarius, symbolised by a centaur. Sagittarius could also be considered the birth sign of cognac since the distilling season starts in late November. Emile also knew his Greek mythology.

Centaurs are creatures, half man and half horse, said by many to symbolise man's dual nature as an intellectual creature (the 'head-in-the-clouds' human half) and a physical animal (the 'feet-on-the-ground' horse half). Sensuality vies with passion. Centaurs were also acolytes of Bacchus, the god of wine.

To Emile, the centaurs' contrasting combination of qualities were also characteristic of cognac: strength (begun in the earth and ending on the palate); mystery (the alchemy of the double distillation process), and ambiguity (its rustic origins but sophisticated maturity).

Rémy Martin's Centaur is Chiron, celebrated for his wisdom and healing abilities and the friend and mentor of Achilles. It also seemed apt to Emile that Chiron's father was Chronos, making him the son of Time itself: a commodity much needed for making fine cognacs.

Emile Rémy Martin had other good reasons for choosing this particular Centaur to represent his company, for Chiron is a visual metaphor of Rémy Martin cognacs in all their contradictory guises from the vineyard to the glass.

On the one hand, they are:

true to tradition
aware of the value of time
wise from centuries of experience
mysterious forces
thoughtful
sharing
individualistic
proud

On the other hand, they are also:

adventurous
impatient to conquer
excited by the future
down-to-earth spirits
dynamic
daring
generous
noble

The Rémy Martin Centaur awakens all the senses to the taste of excellence...

Emile Rémy Martin's choice proved to be an inspired one, not least a century later, in the markets of the Far East. Not only is cognac itself regarded as an aphrodisiac there, but the Chinese, unable to pronounce many Western names, have no trouble asking for *retinomah* – a glass or bottle of 'man-headed horse' cognac. And was it just coincidence that Emile Rémy Martin – though he almost certainly didn't know it – was born in the Chinese year of the horse?

Of course, during the last two centuries, Chiron himself has changed to keep up with changing times. And yet he is still quintessentially himself. Certainly, as Rémy Martin has gone from strength to strength, he has lost none of his abilities. Rather they have been renewed, refined and enhanced.

His big change came in 1966 when he emerged more vital than ever: more of a thoroughbred from the waist down but with the head and broad, muscular torso of a man who was a regular at the gym and worked out with weights. This Chiron's front hooves rear high into the air, looking as though he is about to leap into the heavens and, instead of aiming an arrow at the ground, as he had originally, he is now ready to fling a javelin skywards.

Today, Rémy Martin is indisputably one of the two most important players in the cognac market: a position the Centaur celebrates with panache as he carries his messages of tradition and vision; wisdom and adventure, finesse and taste to the four corners of the globe.

The Perpetuation of Taste...

Cognac is a mysterious spirit in some ways. No-one is really sure why it came into being, and the 'inventor' of distillation, the technique for making cognac, is lost in the mists of history.

Yet in other ways, it is straightforward. Technically, anyone who can grow grapes can distil their wine into brandy. They can grow the same grape varieties, distil in the same way and age their spirit in identical barrels for the same number of years. But they will never be able to produce cognac – and not just for legal reasons.

Everything starts with *terroir*, that untranslatable word which combines the character of the soil, rainfall, sunshine, wind, temperatures and the people who understand these, to give even a tiny region its own distinct identity.

In Cognac, the soil is chalky and crumbly, especially in the *crus*, or regions, of Grande and Petite Champagne. This porous soil can absorb and hold rainfall, releasing it gradually to the vines, but its chalkiness also dictates the types of grapes which will grow well in it. In Cognac, these have varied over the centuries but today there are three main varieties: Ugni Blanc, Colombard and Folle Blanche. Ninety percent of the vineyards are planted with Ugni Blanc.

The rain, as they say in Cognac, falls often but in small amounts, making it wetter than most of France. But the summer days are long and every visitor notices their special light. The sun is never harsh but seems to be filtered through the sky with a gentle luminosity. The chalk soil reflects the light up to the vines and the combination produces a gradual, but regular, ripening of the grapes.

The whole region, but again especially Grande and Petite Champagne, benefits from a special microclimate. Not only does it lie right at the border between northern and southern France but its gentle hills cradle it and protect it from the harsher weather of the Atlantic Ocean to the west and the mountains of central France to the east. So the temperature is generally warm and rarely goes to extremes.

This unique combination has proved perfect for producing cognac. Nowhere else in the world has the same blend of geography and weather and while they may produce a brandy, it will always lack the finesse and complexity of a good cognac.

The gentleness of the landscape and the weather (and 'gentle' is the word everyone applies to all aspects of the region as well as its climate) produces grapes that press into wine which is both acidic and low in alcohol. Not what you want in a glass of white wine. But the levels of both acidity and alcohol are ideal for distilling.

Like all other cognac companies, Rémy Martin buys most of its spirits from independent growers who must respect the company's stringent quality charter. Unlike most, however, for over fifty years it has only bought from the Grande and Petite Champagne regions – the two areas which produce the finest, most intense spirits – where it works in partnership with almost two thousand growers who all abide by its quality charter.

The grapes are crushed and fermented for two weeks before distilling into a clear spirit known as eaux-de-vie. The most aromatic come from wines distilled on their lees (their natural sediments) though the law does not demand this. The lees create the distinctive rich, complex overtones only present in the best cognacs. They also give a greater range of aromas, texture and smoothness to the final cognac. At Rémy Martin all wines are distilled on their lees. Twenty-five pounds of grapes produce about ten quarts of wine which, in turn, distill into only two pints of eaux-de-vie.

The double distillation process demanded by law can be

nerve-wracking. Distilling starts in mid-November and must be completed by 31 March of the next year. During these months you could be blind and deaf and still know you were in Cognac: the rich, grapey aromas from the hundreds of distilleries suffuse the atmosphere. For the distiller, however, it's the liquid dripping from the stills that matters.

Some, like Rémy Martin, only distill in the traditional small *alambic charentais* which holds 2,500 liters (just over 660 gallons) since this has proved to be the size which gives the greatest taste benefits to the eaux-de-vie, concentrating its aromas,

much as a small saucepan reduces broth to a richer glaze than a stock-pot. Also, eaux-de-vie produced in batches are much superior to those produced by continuous stills.

Since the first distillation takes ten to twelve hours and the second, twelve to fourteen, and the still must be thoroughly cleaned after every distillation, the distillery works twenty four hours a day, with the distiller often sleeping on a cot-bed on the premises.

The *alambic charentais*, as its name suggests, is unique to Cognac and they have a magic of their own. Made of copper – and always richly gleaming – they have changed little in three hundred years. The onion-shaped pot still which holds the wine, is firmly bedded in brick above an open fire. Originally wood was used, but today, the heat generally comes from

natural gas: electricity is out because the law decrees the use of flames.

As the wine heats, the alcohol vaporizes and rises through a 'swan's neck' which funnels it down into a swirl of pipes contained in a cooling chamber filled with cold water. As it descends, it condenses into liquid to emerge as a milky

brouillis, or low wine, with an alcohol content of about thirty-percent after the first distillation. The second distillation produces a clear spirit, *la bonne chauffe*, at seventy-percent alcohol by volume.

But not all the eaux-de-vie can be used. The first part in both distillations will be too harsh and the last part too weak. It is the distiller's art to know just where to stop and start. Of course, today's distiller has instruments to help him but most rely just as much on sight, taste and smell as on science.

All new eaux-de-vie are sampled to decide their future life. At Rémy Martin a team of master tasters, men and women of multiple skills, make the decisions. Each possesses the nose and palate to predict the tastes of the future. Their consensus guarantees quality and consistency. To see them at work, either when buying or putting together the components of a final blend, which can contain hundreds of eaux-de-vie (Rémy Martin's best-selling V.S.O.P contains two hundred and forty), is to watch a great art, with each eaux-de-vie making its own mark on the taster's palate and memory bank.

The crystal-clear eaux-de-vie begin their ageing process in new oak barrels. As they mature into cognac, they will be transferred to older barrels. The wood can come from the Limousin or Tronçais forests and the choice is important for the wood will imbue the spirit with tannins, color and subtle flavors. Eaux-de-vie from Grande and Petite Champagne – which are the only ones Rémy Martin buys – require longer ageing than those from other crus to reach their full aromatic complexity. So only wood from eighty-year old Limousin oak trees is used

because it has the wide grain needed to allow the complex tastes of long-maturing cognacs to develop fully.

A visit to the *tonnellerie*, or cooperage, is fascinating and the barrels are almost as important to the final taste of the cognac they contain, as the actual distillation. The 10,000 barrels Rémy Martin needs each year are all hand-crafted on site at the largest traditional cooperage in Europe. Like the barrels the cooperage also makes for Château Petrus, Krug Champagne and Robert Mondavi Opus One, they are made from split oak, which are stacked outdoors to season for at least three years so that any bitter elements can leach out. The classic size holds 350 liters (a little less than 100 gallons): this has proved itself over centuries to produce the best balance between eaux-de-vie's initial, fruity aromas and the subtle aromas it will absorb from the wood.

them at work you know why. No nails or glue can be used. So the thirty two staves that make up each barrel must be fitted together perfectly to prevent leakage. They are first shaped into a 'lampshade' with hoops and then 'toasted' over an open fire of oak chips to help release the flavors and aromas, especially vanilla, which the young eaux-de-vie will absorb on their way to maturity. The 'lampshade' must then be moistened just enough to give it the flexibility to form its final barrel shape. Tops and bottoms are made from oak planks sandwiched together with reeds and fixed with wooden dowels. When attached to the barrel, they are sealed with a flour-and-water 'putty'. It is reckoned that two barrels represent a day's work for one man and, at around $500 each, they are a major investment.

Ageing takes time! Once filled, the barrels are stacked in cel-

lars – though in Cognac, most of these are above ground. The forty two ageing cellars of Rémy Martin shelter six thousand barrels each, containing the largest stock of Fine Champagne Cognac in the world. Made of the local limestone they – like every building holding cognac in barrels – are coated by a fine layer of black fungus. This is *torula cognacensis*, which thrives on the vapors that evaporate through the barrels over the years. This natural evaporation is rather romantically called 'the angels' share' and usually amounts to three percent a year. For Rémy Martin, that means the entire contents of 6,000 barrels disappear every year.

The temperature and humidity of the cellars are carefully controlled as the cognac itself moves from younger to older barrels as it ages. How long that takes depends on the decision of the tasting team which regularly samples the stock, deciding which cognacs should be blended when – and for which of its

brands it should be reserved. Every style of cognac has a minimum age laid down by law: for example, the cognacs blended in any V.S.O.P (Very Superior Old Pale) should be at least four years old, though Rémy Martin age their cognacs considerably longer than required so that they mature to their full potential which, in turn, gives added length to their aftertaste.

Cognac does not improve indefinitely in barrels: thirty to forty years is the maximum for most fine cognacs. But exceptional ones can improve for another fifty and reach their century. Once blended and bottled, there will be no further evaporation, so the cognac will never change.

Time, as we know, is money but Rémy Martin believes that the resulting richness of taste is worth the wait – and the extra cost. Taste, taste and more taste: this is the promise fulfilled by Rémy Martin in all its cognacs. Their floral, fruit and spice notes as well as their richness, complexity and length all combine in a feast of flavors and a memory of lasting pleasure.

Capturing the Spirit of Taste...
From Barrel to Bottle

There are few givens in blending cognac but nothing is haphazard. Each desired style will be a blend of spirits of various ages. But a decisive element in ageing is the cru, from which the spirit comes. The slowest to mature and which also have the greatest potential for development come from Grande and Petite Champagne.

As they mature, amazing transformations take place in the cool silence of the cellars. Unlike other spirits – all of which are distilled from grain and tend to come off the still as raw alcohol – new brandy eaux-de-vie has a floral, fruity aroma which hints at the promise to come. These, called the primary aromas, are the backbone of the spirit which will be fleshed out and colored by spicy nuances, the secondary aromas, absorbed from the barrels as they age.

All eaux-de-vie will be tasted regularly to chart their progress: some will reach their full potential in less than ten years; others can continue to mature for over fifty. The contents of each barrel will be different. And there are almost a quarter of a million barrels of varying ages at Rémy Martin.

The tasting team at Rémy Martin devote their working lives to tasting, day in and day out. They must bring to it a combination of skills: intuition, experience and, perhaps above all, a taste memory of the thousands of different eaux-de-vie. Actually, to call them tasters is something of a misnomer for, since ninety-percent of taste comes from smell, they use their noses much more than their mouths.

The cellarmaster, Georges Clot, and the Master Taster, Vincent Géré, define the styles of the cognacs Rémy Martin makes. M Clot ultimately decides and assembles all the component eaux-de-vie needed for a blend while M. Géré ensures that the style is achieved. Pierrette Trichet, the deputy cellarmaster and one of the very few women in the business, makes sure that as stocks mature, the style can be continued.

Together they compose each *assemblage*, or blend, as an artist uses a palette – in their case, a palette of hundreds of different eaux-de-vie rather than colors – to ensure continuity of style and consistency of taste throughout the range of cognacs. The team also, from time to time, 'invent' new harmonies. Their room is as much a library as a laboratory, though instead of books, the shelves are filled with samples of spirits from different sources and different years all kept for reference. How they achieve this is almost impossible for the layman to grasp. Marrying the different ages and types of spirit can only be done by people with deep knowledge of every aspect of cognac-making from the soil to the final blend.

The Taste Palette of the Rémy Martin Collection...

The six *crus*, or areas, from which cognac can be made have been defined by law since 1909. At about the same time, it was generally recognized that the finest cognacs come from eaux-de-vie made from grapes from the two central crus, Grande Champagne and Petite Champagne.

Only cognacs blended from these two regions and containing at least fifty-percent Grande Champagne can be called Fine Champagne Cognac. All Rémy Martin cognacs are blends from just these two top *crus*. They are also aged considerably longer than required by law.

The result is intensity of taste coupled with a silky smoothness; heady aromas coupled with delicate undernotes, and maturity coupled with liveliness. These characteristics distinguish all Rémy Martin cognacs.

Rémy Martin V.S Grand Cru Cognac

Grand Cru stands at the top of the V.S (Very Special) category of cognacs and is the only V.S to be made from one-hundred-percent Petite Champagne eaux-de-vie. Notes of wild flowers, crisp fruit, vanilla, honey and a hint of mint make an immediate impact on the palate.

It is a party person: lively, fresh, full of life and a good mixer – perfect for long drinks and cocktails as well as neat or on the rocks – an inviting, bright, attractive spirit to be enjoyed before, during and after meals.

Although cognacs need only be aged for two years for this grade of cognac, all those in Rémy Martin's V.S have been aged from three to ten years. It represents the higher standard of V.S cognacs.

Rémy Martin V.S.O.P Fine Champagne Cognac

Critics and connoisseurs alike agree that this is the benchmark of quality against which all other V.S.O.Ps are judged. Not surprisingly, it is the world's favorite – one in three of all bottles of V.S.O.P sold in the world is Rémy Martin – with its distinctive frosted bottle promising a consistently smooth blend of fifty-five-percent Grande and forty-five-percent Petite Champagne cognacs.

It is mature and silky with heady notes of violet and rose; ripe apricots and peaches, vanilla and hazelnuts. These ripe, aromatic flavors are contributed by eaux-de-vie which have been aged in oak barrels from four to fourteen years (none needs be older than four), making it the longest-aged V.S.O.P on the market.

To be drunk neat, on the rocks, or in classic cocktails, V.S.O.P also has enough facets and depth to partner the powerful punch of blue cheeses such as Roquefort, Stilton or Gorgonzola.

Rémy Martin 1738 Accord Royal

One of the most versatile of cognacs, 1738 Accord Royal commemorates the year in which Louis XV broke his own rule forbidding the planting of more vines in Cognac. He made an exception for Rémy Martin, recognising that the company would concentrate on quality not quantity in their eaux-de-vie. He was proved right and today 1738 Accord Royal recreates the rich, authentic, recognizably-different flavors of that time, using the original, closely-guarded method of production. Indeed, its upfront flavors led Georges Clot, who assembled the blend, to nickname it 'Mr More'. The four to twenty year-old eaux-de-vie in the blend are sixty-five-percent Grande Champagne.

The result is a mellow cognac which can be drunk at any time, accompanying a meal or on its own, with or without a cigar. However, its notes of brioche, oak and fruit especially complement chocolate desserts and exotic fruits such as lychees. Then, it should be served at room temperature but 1738 Royal Accord is complex enough to be enjoyed poured over a few ice cubes (which enhance its fruity, floral notes) or served chilled with a splash of sparkling water to bring new distinction to the traditional drink of the region, fine à l'eau – cognac and water.

Rémy Martin X.O Excellence

This Fine Champagne Cognac fully warrants its name with aromatic richness and complexity coming from cognacs aged from ten to thirty-seven years (the law demands no more than seven). Eighty-five-percent of the blend is made up of Grande Champagne cognacs.

The flavors dance in the mouth and the velvet texture and finesse linger long on the palate. Its memorable taste is strikingly fruity, reminiscent of ripe figs and juicy plums with undernotes of toffee and freshly-grated cinnamon.

The excellence and age of this blend with its myriad aromas and opulent richness demand that it be drunk neat though it loses nothing by being served slightly chilled or over ice. Try it with foie gras at the beginning of a meal and as an enhancement to a chocolate dessert.

Rémy Martin Extra

The quintessence of Fine Champagne Cognac, Extra contains ninety-percent Grande Champagne cognacs, all of which are twenty to fifty years old. It is elegant and refined with a harmony of taste that is an aesthetic luxury.

There are complex tones of saffron, sandalwood, walnut and nutmeg and the whiff of a cigar box. Indeed, Extra is a cognac to be enjoyed neat and/or with a good cigar. (Incidentally, cognac and cigars have a longtime association made fashionable in the nineteenth century when the then Prince of Wales, later King Edward VII, preferred to enjoy both in the company of the ladies after dinner, rather than sit for hours with the men over port.)

Distinct and exquisite, the intensity and subtlety, the concentration and fragrance of Extra deserves to be savored slowly.

Louis XIII de Rémy Martin, Grande Champagne Cognac

Undoubtedly the *ne plus ultra* of cognacs – king of spirits and spirit of kings – containing over one thousand eaux-de-vie ranging from forty to one hundred years old. Aged in barrels which themselves are more than a century old, Louis XIII is the unique reward everyone deserves to give themselves at least once in their lives.

Each bottle represents the expertise of three generations of cellarmasters each of which is working for the future pleasure of their grandchildren and great-grandchildren.

A culmination of rare flavors – myrrh, candied fruit, passion fruit, honey and more – Louis XIII is an unforgettable experience, a supreme taste of perfection whose aromas give joy to the palate for over one hour.

This liquid symphony is preserved in an exquisite Baccarat crystal decanter, the faithful reproduction of a Renaissance original found near Cognac over one hundred and fifty years ago. Richly decorated with *fleurs de lys*, the symbol of French royalty, it evokes the sublime spirit within. To be sipped indulgently.

The Taste of Pleasure...

Unlike wine, cognac does not improve in the bottle and bottles should be stored upright. There is no point in not drinking it once you've bought it. The widely-held idea that the old, cobwebby bottle will contain something finer than a clean new one has no merit.

In Evelyn Waugh's *Brideshead Revisited*, Charles Ryder, the narrator, dines the upstart Rex Mottram at a famous Paris restaurant (easily identifiable as La Tour d'Argent). Pale, delicate cognac is poured from a clean bottle '*...free from grime and Napoleonic cyphers. It was only a year or two older than Rex and lately bottled. They gave it to us in very thin tulip-shaped glasses of modest size...*'

Rex thinks he is being patronized and insists on a huge bal-loon glass warmed over a spirit lamp. So, '...*shamefacedly, they wheeled out of its hiding place, the vast and mouldy bottle they kept for people of Rex's sort. It was a treacly concoction which left dark rings around the side of his glass... a ballon the size of his head. "That's the stuff", he said'.* Although Ryder, like Waugh himself, was an insufferable snob, this admirably describes how – and how not to – drink fine cognac.

Of course, standard-size balloon glasses are fine, especially for an after-dinner cognac, but tulip-shaped 'cellarmaster' glasses make good alternatives, and the thin crystal glasses specially-designed for the 'Only Rémy' Dinners add elegance to any table when cognacs are to be drunk throughout a meal.

The Pleasures of Taste...
The Only Rémy Dinners- *In The Spirit of Excellence*

The Only Rémy Dinners were conceived in a spirit of adven-ture. They are serious but should be fun. A brainstorming ses-sion at Rémy Martin's headquarters in Cognac came up with the idea of pairing their cognacs with food. Cognac is a distillate of wine, they reasoned, and whole books are devoted to pairing them. It was already known that cognacs make good friends with chocolate and coffee. And, although cognac is the perfect finish to a fine dinner, why should it be relegated to the end of the meal?

Why not, they thought, ask some of the world's top chefs to experiment to develop menus in which a cognac would work well with every dish? Naturally enough, they started in France and, naturally enough, there was some scepticism at first. But Rémy Martin made it clear right from the start that the chefs had *carte blanche*.

A few weeks into the scheme, and obviously expecting to be accused of heresy, a much-Michelin-starred chef called HQ. Could he, he asked nervously, try chilling the cognacs? 'You can put them in the freezer if you like', was the unexpected reply. So he did. (The alcohol prevents the liquid from freezing solid.) The results were exceptional and added yet more possibilities to be researched.

Some notable menus were created. But France is France and French food is still based on tradition. To really explore all the possibilities, Rémy Martin decided to go abroad. And where else but the United States where some of the most adventurous combinations of food are served and rules are made to be broken (or at least questioned)?

It was by pure coincidence that the publisher of *First Impressions of International Dining*, David Shaw, had decided to approach some of America's greatest chefs. His proposal to them was to produce a definitive guide book covering signature dishes of celebrated restaurants. A successful series of meetings result-ed in this joint production, "The Spirit of Excellence".

Thirty of the chefs approached by David and who have taken up the challenge in this book are among the best and most cre-ative in the United States and Rémy Martin congratulates them on their inventiveness and flair. Obviously, they have individual-ly discovered some common themes: foie gras, shellfish and blue cheeses all turn out to be spectacular partners of cognacs. But there is also a fascinating variety in the pairings, in some of which, the dish and cognac are complementary, while in others, their tastes contrast. Both are equally valid.

You can, of course, prove this for yourself by simply visiting the restaurants of these chefs when they present the "In the Spirit of Excellence" concept on their menus. But you will also want to cook many of the mouthwatering dishes in these pages, so why not organize your own "In the Spirit of Excellence" dinner for a special occasion? The first thing to remember is that it should be fun and the chefs have done all the hard work for you, including choosing which cognac they think makes the perfect match with each dish. Do you agree with them?

Vincent Géré, the chief taster at Rémy Martin, has devoted many months to working out the perfect formula for making the most of an "Only Rémy Dinner" and, certainly to start with, it's well worth following his advice on how to taste your way through the meal, whether ordered in one of the restaurants in this book or at your own dinner party. Both should be relaxed occasions but there are certain rituals which will make them special and even more enjoyable.

"This is the Rémy Martin that we know today. A company born from a dream and perfected over time. A company of two histories – each forever synonymous with the other."

Advice on the Pairing of Cognac with Food

As far as tasting is concerned, it is worth taking your time. An Only Rémy Dinner can feature a range of three to five cognacs. If it's a very special evening and a glass of Louis XIII is served after the meal, it becomes the Ultimate Rémy Dinner and a supreme indulgence. (In the United States these already happen annually when Rémy Martin hosts a dinner for the James Beard Foundation with part of the proceeds going to the charity.)

"First of all," says **Mr Géré**, *"unwind. Depending on the number of courses served, you will be consuming less alcohol than if you drank two glasses of wine and you will be tasting the best Fine Champagne cognacs alongside dishes specifically created for them. It is a voyage of discovery and one of the most exciting things is that, because each cognac is a blend of anywhere from two hundred and forty to six hundred different eaux-de-vie, different notes or facets come to the fore at different times depending on what each is drunk with and even at which temperature – ambient, chilled or fresh from the freezer – it is served. The different reactions with different foods really do help you understand the complexities of aromas contained in any one Rémy Martin cognac."*

For example, Gale Gand of Tru, in Chicago and Richard Reddington of L'Auberge du Soleil, in the Napa Valley, go the chocolate route with a rich chocolate malted semifreddo (from her) and a chocolate-on-chocolate cake (from him) paired with 1738 Royal Accord. Michael Patton of Brix, in the Napa Valley,

is most adventurous with complex flavor combinations in his oxtail, wild mushroom and leek fricassée served on truffle polenta and paired with X.O Excellence. In fact, it is interesting to see how many of the chefs have found successful pairings with one of Rémy Martin's cogancs and meat. Foie gras, of course, makes several appearances.

Elsewhere, an iced Rémy Martin V.S, with its hints of vanilla and mint, may be served with a ceviche of thinly-sliced scallops; a brochette of langoustines and monkfish with a saffron sauce is enhanced by the same note of saffron in Rémy Martin Extra served chilled; the ripe fruit flavors of chilled Rémy Martin X.O bring out the best in pigeon breasts spiced Chinese-style, while the same cognac, served at room temperature, shows that its rich cinnamon and hazelnut aromas stand up to a strong, aged hard cheese, and Rémy Martin's best-selling V.S.O.P brings the contrast of liquorice and the complement of apricots to a lemon meringue tart with apricot sorbet.

But back to *your* tasting. To get the most out of a fine cognac, it's worth indulging in some ritual. First, look at the cognac. Many people think that the darker the cognac, the older it will be. But don't be fooled: this is not true. Swirl the glass gently and examine the traces, or 'legs', of liquid as they slide back to base. They should slip down limpidly.

"Slowly bring the glass to your nose", says Vincent Géré, *"rather than your nose to the glass. As it approaches, inhale several times. As it gets closer, fruit and floral aromas will make their appearance. As the glass reaches the nose, spice notes will join them. Take the time to appreciate them as their emphases change. A good cognac will immediately release a pleasant freshness and balanced fruitiness. The mature cognac will also start to release the complexity of the aromas it has absorbed from the oak barrels: spicy notes with wood and vanilla overtones.*

Now taste, in small sips allowing the cognac to spread out in the mouth towards the back where the most sensitive tastebuds live. Now, nuts and oak flavors will come to the fore. The finer and longer the taste remains on the back palate, the better the finish. The amazing complexities of aromas and refinements of flavors in Rémy Martin's cognacs are like an explosion in the mouth.

Take your first taste of the dish in front of you and appreciate the complexities and harmony of its ingredients. Now you can combine sips of the cognac with bites of the food. Your palate will find it surprisingly easy to recognize a changing kaleidoscope of taste. A good pairing, like Rémy Martin cognacs, is always more than the sum of its parts, taking them to a higher level. All flavors are intensified and bring out the best in each other. Each of you at the table may – in fact, almost certainly will – have different opinions of the pairings. But that is as it should be. By the end of the meal, you will truly understand the meaning of our French phrase 'chacun a son gout'!"

Chef Sandro Gamba

N O M I

About the Chef...

A French native, **Sandro Gamba** has worked extensively in both France and the United States. Most recently, he served at *Lespinasse*, located in the Hotel St. Regis, D.C. and also has trained with Alain Ducasse during his tenure at *Le Louis XV*, Joel Robuchon at *Le Jamin* and with Roger Verge at *Le Moulin de Mougins*. His cuisine is light yet reminiscent of the home-cooked meals he fondly recounts and has, in fact, duplicated in a breakfast called *'Grandmother Geannette's Breakfast.'*

In addition to being honored with a nomination as the 1999 *James Beard Rising Star award*, Gamba has earned a Five Star Rating and was selected as one of the *World's Best Chefs* by the American Academy of Hospitality Sciences in 1999 for Lespinasse, which also picked up the Five Diamonds from AAA.

About the Restaurant...

The view is breathtaking at breakfast, lunch or dinner, but if you're fortunate enough to be seated at twilight, you'll be entranced by fifteen minutes of piercing blue light, that seeps through the sloping floor-to-ceiling bay windows of *NoMI*. It's the final transformation of day into night, and it's one of those single moments that should be captured in a glass jar and preserved forever.

Executive chef Sandro Gamba relishes this time daily. His restaurant proudly looks out on the city's jewels, like a mother keeping watch over her children, seven floors above the prestigious North Michigan Street. With unobstructed views of the Miracle Mile and the vast Lake Michigan, a table in this dining room is like having a front row seat to the best show in town.

But Chef Gamba's eyes focus on another view. The French native surveys the crowd, ranging from hip young socialites to business travelers and celebrities, from his full theatre kitchen. Presented on stage is an elegant display of French and Japanese culinary dishes ranging from melt-in-your-mouth sashimi, Pork Terrine with braised chestnuts, foie gras, apricots and a fig and artichoke salad, to Sautéed Veal Sweetbreads, in a vibrantly coloured ragout of fresh peas, morels, pearl onion, herb spatzle and English Peas Veloute. Worthy, indeed, of display in the Chicago Museum of Contemporary Art.

NoMI's artistic ambiance, in tune with Chicago's passion for art and culture, is evident throughout the restaurant. The presentation of food is graceful, sophisticated and yet astonishingly clean and simple. The design of the restaurant unfolds from a 3,000 bottle wine cellar to a bar lounge, which opens up to the sleek and minimalist dining room. The walls are decorated with works from such masters as Gerhard Richter, Isamu Noguchi, and Dale Chihuly, adding the final finishing touches to this artist's palette.

Frozen Vanilla Raspberry Bavarian Bombe

PAIRED WITH RÉMY LOUIS XIII

INGREDIENTS

Raspberry Sorbet
36 oz. Fresh Raspberry Puree
9 oz. Granulated Sugar
16 oz. Water
1 tsp. Lemon Juice
1 oz. Honey

Sablee
7 oz. Butter
7 oz. All purpose flour
3 oz. Confectioners sugar
1 pinch Salt
1 Whole egg

Vanilla Bavarian
8 oz. Whole milk
2 Vanilla beans
7 oz. Granulated sugar
8 Egg yolks
17 oz. Cream

Red wine reduction
1 bottle red wine
1 cup Raspberries
1 cup Blueberries
1 cup Blackberries
1 cup Strawberries
1/2 cup
1 Sugar Bay leaf

METHOD

Raspberry Sorbet:
Bring water, sugar and honey to quick boil. Allow to cool and add fruit pieces and lemon juice and freeze in a machine. Place finished product into small mold that will fit inside bombe.

Sablee:
Combine butter and sugar in a mixing bowl. Mix until creamy. Add salt and the egg and mix. Last, add flour gently mixing until dough comes together. Wrap in plastic wrap and refrigerate. Roll dough to a thickness of 1/4" and cut to fit the bottom of the bombe mold (a bowl, container, etc.) Bake the sable on 320°f for about 8 minutes. Reserve.

Vanilla Bavarian:
Combine sugar and yolks, immediately mix with a whisk. Bring milk and vanilla beans to boil and slowly pour over sugar/yolk mixture. Return mixture to heat and cook until thickens slightly. Cool completely. While cooling mixture, whip cream until stiff and fold into cold custard.

Assembly:
Pour Bavarian into desired mold. Place a disc of raspberry sorbet into Bavarian, careful not to push to the bottom of mold *(which will eventually be the top)*. Place a disc of sable on bottom and place in freezer for at least six hours. Serve with a red wine berry reduction.

Red wine reduction:
Combine ingredients and simmer until wine thickens and coats the back of a spoon.
Strain and refrigerate until needed.

Roasted Veal Loin and Sweetbreads

WITH RAGOUT OF PEAS, MORELS, AND PEARL ONIONS, PEA FOAM.
PAIRED WITH RÉMY EXTRA

METHOD

For the Sweetbreads:

Cover Sweetbreads in port and Madeira 1 to 1 ratio. Let marinate overnight. Place sweetbreads in large pot to hold in single layer. Add 1 carrot, 1 celery stalk, 1 onion cut in large dice, 1 bunch thyme, 1 bay leaf, 8 black peppercorns. In separate pot, place port and Madeira. Reduce by half. Add this to sweetbreads and cover the rest with chicken stock. Bring to simmer and let cook until sweetbreads are slightly firm, medium-rare. Pull out and let cool. Cut these in 2 oz. portions.

For the foam:

Put $1^1/_2$ lbs peas in a pot and cover with chicken stock. Let cook on medium heat until tender. Puree in blender. Foam in handblender with 1 tbsp olive oil and 1 tbsp butter and salt and pepper.

For the morels:

Sweat 2 diced shallots and $^1/_4$ cup brunoise ham in a pot. Add morels and cover with chicken stock and 1 tbsp butter, and 1 tbsp olive oil. Cook on low heat until tender.

For the pearl onions:

Sauté onions in olive oil until slight color. Cover in chicken stock and add 1 tbsp butter in olive oil.

For the spaetzle:

Mix $1^1/_2$ cups milk with 3 eggs. In mixer, combine on medium speed with 3 cups flour, and a pinch of nutmeg, and salt and pepper. Let dough rest for an hour. Using a Spätzhobel, cook the spaetzle in boiling salted water until they float. Pull out of the water and shock in ice water. Reserve.

To cook:

Sauté veal and sweetbreads in olive oil. Heat onions, fresh peas, and morels in olive oil, butter and chicken stock. Season with salt and pepper. Heat pea sauce and foam with hand blender. Sauté the spaelzle in small dollop of butter until golden and season with salt and pepper. Place ragout on plate, place veal and sweetbreads on top, and spoon sauce around all. Spread spaetzle around veal in foam.

INGREDIENTS

8 Veal Medallions, $2^1/_2$ oz.
2 lb. Fresh Shucked Peas
1 lb. Fresh Morels
20 White Pearl Onions, Cleaned
2 Large Veal Sweetbreads
20 Herb Spaetzle
1 Carrot
1 Celery Stalk
1 Onion
1 Bunch Thyme
1 Bayleaf
Port
Madeira Wine

Chefs Rick Tramonto & Gale Gand

T R U

About the Chefs...

Rick Tramonto's 21-year restaurant career has been a climb to the stars. With the stellar success of *Tru*, open since May 1999, Tramonto is a star in his own right. His credits are myriad. Tru was nominated by the James Beard Foundation, 2001 – Best Chef: Midwest, 2000 – Best New Restaurant. In 2000, *Condé Nast Traveler's* Top 50 best Restaurants in the World, in 1994, *Food & Wine's* Top Ten Best New Chefs in the country. He has also been on *Oprah*.

He met partner Gale Gand at Strathallen. He worked with Gerard Pangaud at *Aurora*. In Chicago, he worked at *Avanzare*, and *Scoozi!* before moving to a successful stint at five-star *Stapleford Park Hotel*, as well as the *Criterion Brasserie*, in England, receiving the coveted Michelin Guide's Red "M" at Stapleford – a rare feat, indeed. After working with the world's greatest chefs, including Anton Mosimann, Michel Guerard, and Raymond Blanc, he and Gale returned to Chicago in 1993.

When six, **Gale Gand** caught the lens of a *Life* magazine photographer while she was making mud pies. Thirty-some years later, the ingredients may have changed, but she is still catching the eyes and tastes of all those who witness her latest creations. 2001 marked the year that Gand received the James Beard Foundation Award for Outstanding Pastry Chef. Other major accolades include *Bon Appetit's* annual Best of the Best awards for 2001, the Robert Mondavi Award for Culinary Excellence 1994, with Rick Tramonto –the Top Ten Best New Chefs by *Food & Wine*, the 1998 James Beard Award for Best Chefs in the Midwest, nominations for the 2000 James Beard Award with Tru for the Best New Restaurant and also Outstanding Pastry Chef.

International critics such as Fay Maschler of the *London Evening Standard* called Gand's ice creams "the best I have tasted in Britain."

About the Restaurant...

"Beauty is truth, truth beauty, that is all ye know on earth and all ye need to know." **John Keats 1795-1821,** *Ode On A Grecian Urn.*

After a dining experience at **TRU**, you'll agree that nothing could capture the concept of this restaurant better than Keats' words. The name "TRU" comes from Executive Chef Rick Tramonto and Pastry Chef Gale Gand's absolute determination to be true to their art – and the result is sheer beauty. The restaurant, located in downtown Chicago, welcomes its guests through rich black and white drapes into a huge white dining room, with splashes of blue from art such as the *Venus Bleue*, and from blue velvet "purse stools", conveniently positioned next to each chair.

The *Warhol* on the wall is almost dwarfed next to Tramonto's creations, which are served on unusual surfaces, all in the name of fun. His Caviar Glass Staircase, for example, is a rainbow of Golden Whitefish Roe, Wasabi Roe, Sea Trout Roe and Iranian Sevruga, or you can really "push the boat out" and opt for the sultry, All Black Caviar Staircase. Innovative entrees from the prix- fixe progressive French menu, include Espresso Crusted Millbrook Farm Venison Loin, with braised red cabbage, while veggie-lovers can enjoy Goat Cheese Tortellini, with red onion jam, and chive emulsion.

The food, ambiance and decor complement one another perfectly, but it would not be TRU without the perfect ending to a truly memorable meal – a dessert from Gale Gand's stunning selection. An excellent choice is the Sticky Toffee Date Cake with roasted apricots and vanilla-brandy ice cream. But with a TV show, numerous cook books, and the highly coveted James Beard Award for Outstanding Pastry Chef all under her belt, you can understand why her Chocolate Malted Semifreddo, with anise scented oranges and 24K syrup, presented in the shape of a shooting star, captures this shining constellation so brilliantly.

Malaysian Rack of Lamb

PAIRED WITH RÉMY VSOP

INGREDIENTS

6 oz. Lamb Chops
2 oz. Green Cauliflower Puree
1/4 oz. Bread Pudding
1 oz. White Cauliflower- Quartered
2 oz. Lamb Sauce
1/2 oz. Truffle Vinaigrette
1 oz. Swiss Chard

Marinade
5 tbsp. oyster sauce
2 tbsp. soy sauce
3 tbsp. rice wine vinegar
3 tbsp. sesame oil
1/2 cup olive oil
1 tbsp. chili
1 tbsp. fish sauce

Bread and Butter Pudding
1 Loaf Brioche
12 oz. Vidalia Onion
1 oz. Black Truffle Oil
1/2 oz. Clarified Butter
2 oz. Madeira
Salt and Pepper To Taste
Custard

Bread Pudding Custard
5 Cups Heavy Cream
3 Cups Half and Half
18 Egg Yolks
2 oz. Shallot
1/4 oz. Garlic
Sprig Of Thyme
Rosemary
1 oz. Clarified Butter
Salt and Pepper To Taste

Red Wine Sauce
4 oz. Shallot
4 oz. Garlic
1 Cup Carrots
1 Cup Celery
32 oz. Red Wine
3 Thyme Sprigs
128 oz. Veal Demi-Glace

Brioche Dough
Yields: 1 large fish box
2 1/2 oz. Fresh Yeast
2 1/2 oz. Warm Water
3 LB. 5 oz. All Purpose Flour
3 LB. 5 oz. High Gluten Flour
2 oz. Salt
9 oz. Sugar
30 Eggs
4 Lb. Butter, Cold and Cut Up

METHOD

Malaysian Rack of Lamb: Cook lamb rack to desired doneness. Quenelle puree and place cauliflower that has been caramelized in butter on end of quenelle. Heat pudding in oven. Place next to quenelle. Sauté Swiss chard in butter and place in center of plate. Slice rack into chops and place three chops onto Swiss chard. Sauce around chops and drizzle vinaigrette around bread pudding.

Marinade: Whisk all ingredients into bowl. Marinate lamb rack for at least three hours.

Bread and Butter Pudding: Trim crust off brioche. Cube into 1/4" cubes. Toast lightly in oven for 10 minutes. Caramelize onion until deep amber in color. Deglaze with Madeira and reduce to sec. Soak brioche in liberal amount of custard. Add truffle oil. Let rest - soak overnight. Layer in shallow 1/2 hotel pan. Top with more custard. Bake for 40-45 minutes in water bath at 300°f in conventional oven.

Bread Pudding Custard: Toast shallot, garlic and herbs lightly. Add cream and half & half. Bring to boil. Temper cream mixture into egg yolks. Season with salt and pepper. Strain through chinois and chill.

Red Wine Sauce: Caramelize vegetables. Add wine and thyme and reduce to au sec. Add veal glace and simmer until sauce consistency. Strain and cool. Refrigerate.

Brioche Dough: Dissolve yeast in warm water. Place dry ingredients in mixer with a dough hook; mix on low to combine. Add eggs and dissolved yeast, continue mixing to combine. Add cut up butter; mix till you no longer see pieces of butter. Turn dough into a plastic container and cover. Chill overnight.

For thin loaves: Scale out 1 1/8 lbs. of dough and shape into a long log. Place in pan, cover with plastic wrap and proof till dough reaches the top of the pan. Remove plastic and bake at 325°f in convection oven for 25 minutes, rotating after 10 minutes. Remove from pans immediately and let cool on a wire rack.

For large loaves: Scale out 2 1/4 lbs. of dough and shape into a long log. Place in pan, cover with plastic wrap and proof till dough reaches the top of pan. Remove plastic and bake at 350°f in convection oven for 45 minutes, rotating after 20 minutes. Remove from pans immediately and let cool on a wire rack.

For mini loaves: Scale out 1/2 oz. balls and place 3 in each pan side by side. Cover with plastic wrap and proof till dough reaches the top of the pan about 1 hour and 15 minutes. Remove plastic and bake in a convection oven at 325°f for 13-16 minutes

Caviar

Caviar

PAIRED WITH RÉMY XO EXCELLENCE

INGREDIENTS

½ oz. Beluga
½ oz. Tobiko
½ oz. Wasabi
½ oz. White Fish
1 Whole Egg – Hard boiled and chopped white
    and yolk separated
½ oz. Capers, Chopped
½ oz. Red Onion, Minced, Rinsed In Cold Water
3 oz. Crème Fraîche
10 Each Brioche, Sliced And Toasted
    Chives, Chopped

M E T H O D

Chocolate Malted Semi Freddo

PAIRED WITH RÉMY 1738

INGREDIENTS

4 Yolks
½ Scant Cup Sugar
2 Tbsp. Brandy
2 Tbsp. Malt Powder
⅓ Cup Milk
½ Vanilla Bean, Split
½ Cup Semi Sweet Valrhona Chocolate Pistols
1¾ Cups Heavy Cream, Whipped To Soft Peaks
Serves 8

M E T H O D

Line round 2½" inch collars with strips of acetate and place them in the freezer. In a large bowl whisk together yolks, sugar, brandy, malt powder, milk and vanilla bean over a hot water bath cook whisking constantly till very thick, like a sabayon. Remove from heat. Take out vanilla bean. Whisk in chocolate to melt it, let this cool almost completely. Fold in whipped cream until completely combined. Pour semifreddo mixture into collars filling ⅛" from top and freeze over night. To serve, take out of the collar and sprinkle lightly with cocoa powder and powdered sugar. Place on dessert plates, peel off acetate. Let sit for 10 minutes before serving to temper it.

Preparation time: 20 minutes -
Cooking time: 10 minutes - Ease of preparation: moderate

Chef Carlos E. Rodriguez

PAPPAS BROS. STEAKHOUSE

About the Chef...

The oldest son of a career U.S. Air Force Officer, **Carlos Rodriguez** spent his childhood traveling across the United States, Europe, and South America. His exposure to vastly different cultures and, more importantly, radically different cuisines, formed the foundation of his passion for cooking.

For the past fourteen years, Carlos has been fortunate enough to indulge this passion full-time, working for some of the finest restaurants, and chefs Texas has to offer.

In 1993 Rodriguez graduated with honors from Le Chef Culinary Arts School in Austin, Texas. From there he went on to work at *Frisch Auf Valley Country Club*, Rio Ranch, and *Post Oak Grill* before becoming Executive Chef at *Pappas Bros. Steakhouse* in Dallas.

About the Restaurant...

"A gourmet who thinks of calories is like a tart who looks at her watch." James Beard.

With a menu that features thirty two-ounce Porterhouse Steaks and towers of bagel-sized onion rings, a forty eight- page wine list featuring some fifteen hundred selections of wine, and an extraordinarily large, labyrinthine restaurant with giant pillars and expansive marble surfaces, you'd better believe that at **Pappas Bros. Steakhouse**, size does matter!

In business for over 60 years, the Pappas family have certainly outdone themselves with the

opening of this fine-dining establishment, serving dry-aged prime beef. As you walk into the main dining room, you feel immediately transported into "the Roaring Twenties", replete with rich leather booths, marble columns, and mahogany paneling. The opulent surroundings, redolent of a James Cagney, gangster-movie era, make you want to spend all your money on the biggest steak in the house and Executive Chef Carlos helps you ease that craving. Since 1998 Rodriguez has been feeding Dallas, the third largest prime beef market in the US, with some of the most sought-after steak in the country.

The menu is unapologetically minimalist, presenting a la carte steak items seasoned simply with kosher salt, black pepper and butter to draw out the rich taste. The Fresh Asparagus, Roasted Wild Mushrooms, or Mashed Potatoes are all satisfying sides, but I've always believed that nothing goes better with a great steak than a good bottle of red wine, and you certainly have pick of the choice at this place. If you can manage an appetizer, the Bacon-wrapped Scallops or the Beefsteak Tomato with onions and Roquefort cheese are both exceptional choices.

But Pappas Bros. is more than just a dining experience – be sure to stop in the cigar lounge and choose from over sixty brands and sizes before you call it a night.

Prosciutto — Wrapped Buffalo Tenderloin

WITH IRON SKILLET POTATOES AND HARICOT VERT, TOPPED WITH SEARED FOIE GRAS
AND PORT WINE SHIITAKE MUSHROOM SAUCE. PAIRED WITH RÉMY XO EXCELLENCE

INGREDIENTS

Sauce
2 Cups Mirepoix
1/2 Cup Olive Oil
4 Cups Port Wine
2 Cups Veal Stock
2 Ea. Bay Leaves
2 Cups Shiitake
Mushrooms Sliced and
Cooked, *As Needed Kosher
Salt and Black Pepper*

Iron Skillet Potatoes
2 Ea. Cooked Idaho
Potatoes, Peeled and
Thickly Sliced
1 Cup Caramelized Yellow
Onions
1/4 Cup Chives, Chopped
1/4 Cup Bacon, Chopped
Fine
*As Needed Kosher Salt and
White Pepper*

Buffalo
1 Ea. 8 oz. Buffalo
Tenderloin
1 Ea. Thin Sliced Aged
Prosciutto (Can Substitute
Bacon)
*As Needed Kosher Salt and
Pepper*
2 oz. Foie Gras, Seared

METHOD

Sauce:
In saucepot, caramelize Mirepoix in olive oil. Drain off excess oil, add port wine and Bay Leaves, reduce by 1/2. Add veal stock and reduce by 1/2. Strain sauce, return to heat and add mushrooms. Simmer 10 minutes or until thickened to nappe. Adjust seasoning with Salt and Pepper.

Iron Skillet Potatoes:
Heat a cast iron skillet until smoking. Reduce heat, add diced bacon and cook until fat is rendered. Add potatoes, cook 2-3 minutes more until browned on other side. Add caramelized onions, toss to combine. Season with Salt and Pepper, add chives at service (this preserves the chives' color)

Buffalo:
Wrap tenderloin with Prosciutto and secure with steak pin or toothpick. Season liberally with Kosher Salt and Black Pepper. Grill to desired doneness. In a hot pan, sear Foie Gras on both sides until outside is crispy and warmed throughout.

Chilled Main Lobster

WITH MANGO AND CUCUMBER SALAD WITH SWEET MISO VINAIGRETTE. PAIRED WITH RÉMY EXTRA

METHOD

Vinaigrette:

Combine Miso, Champagne Vinegar, Honey, Mustard, Garlic, Basil and Shallots in blender or food processor. Pulse until combined. On low speed, slowly add olive oil until Vinaigrette is emulsified. Adjust seasoning with salt and pepper, add lemon juice.

Salad:

Combine diced mangos and diced cucumbers in bowl. Clip lobster meat from arms and add. Season with Kosher salt and fresh ground pepper to taste, add vinaigrette to moisten.

Plating:

Drizzle vinaigrette on to chilled plate. Slice Lobster tail meat on the bias, shingle on center of plate. Place claws on the plate. Reserve head and tailfins for garnish. Using a ring mold, place 1/4 - 1/2 cup mango salad in mold, press down to hold shape and remove mold. Top salad with baby field greens tossed in vinaigrette. Place head standing up between claws. Place the fins at base of the sliced tail meat. Drizzle aged Balsamic Vinegar around place. Serve chilled.

INGREDIENTS

1 Ea. 2-3 Lbs. Main Lobster, Cooked Chilled, Shelled	1/2 Tsp. Dijon Mustard
1 Ea. Mango, Ripe, Diced	2 Tbsp. Honey
1 Ea. English Cucumber, Seeded, Diced – Salad	1 Clove Garlic
1 Tbsp. Chives, Minced	1 Tbsp. Basil, Chopped
3 Tbsp. Blonde Miso	1 Cup Olive Oil
Vinaigrette	1/4 Tsp. Shallots, Minced
1/3 Cup Champagne Vinegar	Juice Of 1 Lemon
	To Taste Kosher Salt and Black Pepper

INGREDIENTS

Sabayon

12 Egg Yolks
3/4 Cup Granulated Sugar
1 1/4 oz. Rémy Martin XO Excellence Cognac

Rémy Martin XOE Sabayon

WITH FRESH BERRIES, PAIRED WITH RÉMY LOUIS XIII

METHOD

In stainless steel bowl, combine egg yolks and sugar. Whip vigorously until slightly fluffy. Add Cognac and combine. Over a bain marie, whip mixture until it begins to thicken and falls in ribbons. Remove from heat, continue whipping over an ice bath until well chilled and becomes shiny.

To serve:

In 10 oz. Martini Glass, fill 3/4 of glass with fresh sliced strawberries, raspberries and blackberries. Spoon Sabayon into dish to cover. Top with fresh whipped cream and more berries.

Chef William A. Koval

Dallas

About the Chef...

William A. Koval earned international acclaim at the Ritz-Carlton Hotel Company by becoming its youngest executive chef at 25. He took over at The Adolphus in 1994. Since his arrival, *The French Room* was named one of America's "Top Tables" *(Gourmet)* for three consecutive years, "Twenty-five Best Dining Experiences in the World" *(Travel & Leisure)*, in Zagat, has earned "29" a near-perfect score, making it an elite group member of only nine restaurants to achieve it nationwide.

William Koval is the resident chef WFAA-TV Channel 8's *Good Morning Texas*. He was an American culinary gold medallist at the 2002 Winter Olympics in Salt Lake City. Much of his success was due to the recommendation by his mentor Franz Mitterer, Ritz-Carlton Corporate Chef who sent him to Hotel Le Bristol in Paris where he distinguished himself under the Michelin grand master chefs.

Koval, who graduated in the top 5% of his class at the CIA in 1981, is a native of Waterbury, Connecticut. He is married with three children.

About the Restaurant...

Prepare yourself for a sensory overload as you enter Dallas' top rated restaurant, **The French Room**. Located inside the Beaux-Arts style Hotel Adolphus built in 1912, the French Room is as much a feast for the eyes as the classic cuisine is for the palate. A Cathedral-like vaulted ceiling mural by Alexandra Rosenfield crowns the room with rosy-cheeked cherubs, pale blue skies and clouds embellished by gilded Rococo arches and a stunning hand-blown crystal chandelier.

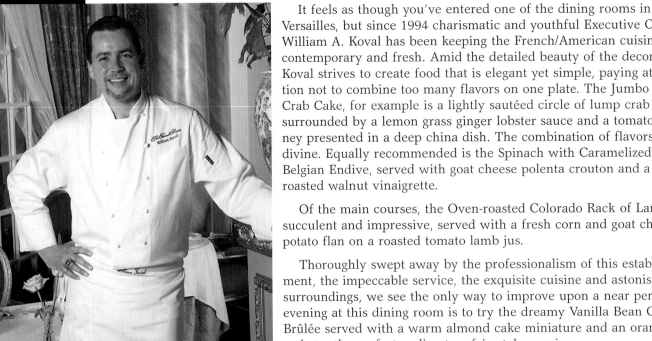

It feels as though you've entered one of the dining rooms in Versailles, but since 1994 charismatic and youthful Executive Chef William A. Koval has been keeping the French/American cuisine contemporary and fresh. Amid the detailed beauty of the decor, Koval strives to create food that is elegant yet simple, paying attention not to combine too many flavors on one plate. The Jumbo Lump Crab Cake, for example is a lightly sautéed circle of lump crab meat surrounded by a lemon grass ginger lobster sauce and a tomato chutney presented in a deep china dish. The combination of flavors is divine. Equally recommended is the Spinach with Caramelized Belgian Endive, served with goat cheese polenta crouton and a roasted walnut vinaigrette.

Of the main courses, the Oven-roasted Colorado Rack of Lamb is succulent and impressive, served with a fresh corn and goat cheese potato flan on a roasted tomato lamb jus.

Thoroughly swept away by the professionalism of this establishment, the impeccable service, the exquisite cuisine and astonishing surroundings, we see the only way to improve upon a near perfect evening at this dining room is to try the dreamy Vanilla Bean Crème Brûlée served with a warm almond cake miniature and an orange sorbet – the perfect ending to a fairy-tale evening.

Oven Roasted Lamb

Lamb

WITH A ROASTED TOMATO, ROSEMARY AND GARLIC SAUCE WITH CORN TURTLETS.
PAIRED WITH RÉMY 1738

INGREDIENTS

Lamb Stock
20 Lbs. Lamb Bones, Roasted
1 Onion, Rough Chopped
2 Carrots, Rough Chopped
4 Stalks Celery, Rough Chopped
5 Black Peppercorns
2 Tbsp. Tomato Paste

Lamb Sauce
4 Cloves Garlic, Roasted
2 Shallots, Chopped
1 Bottle Pinot Noir
1 Gallon Lamb Stock
5 Black Peppercorns
2 Sprigs Fresh Type
1 Sprig Fresh Rosemary

Roasted Tomato Lamb Sauce
5 Roma Tomatoes, Cut In Half
2 Shallots
2 Cloves Garlic
3 Tbsp. Olive Oil
2 Sprigs Rosemary
Salt and Pepper To Taste

Lamb Starch
3 Medium-Sized Potatoes, Cooked Halfway, Cooled, Peeled, Grated Large Whole
3 Ears Fresh Corn (Remove Kernels)
3 Shallots Small, Diced
2 Strips Bacon, Smoked, Small Dice
2 Sprigs Fresh Thyme, Leaves Removed
2 Tbsp. Olive Oil
6 Molds (4 oz) Sprayed or Buttered
6 oz. Bucheron Chevre
Salt and Pepper

Make custard
4 Whole Eggs
2 Cups Heavy Cream
Salt and Pepper

METHOD

Lamb:
Season with salt and pepper. Sear all sides in a sauté pan until golden brown. Finish in 350°f oven until desired temperature is reached.

Lamb Stock:
Roast lamb bones until well browned on all sides. Roast onions, carrots, celery until well browned. Allow to cool overnight. Assemble bones and vegetables in heavy stainless steel kettle or stockpot. Add cold water, tomato paste and peppercorns. Bring to boil, simmer for six hours. Strain through china cap.

Lamb Sauce:
Reduce wine with garlic, shallots and peppercorns by 80%. Add lamb stock and bring to boil. Reduce heat and simmer until reduced to desired consistency. Remove from heat. Steep fresh thyme and rosemary in finished sauce for 15-20 minutes. Strain through fine mesh chinois.

Roasted Tomato Lamb Sauce:
Mix ingredients together and roast in over at 350°f until brown. Remove from oven, puree in blender and strain. Add to lamb sauce until desired taste is acquired.

Lamb Starch:
In a sauté pan, add olive oil and heat. Add bacon and render, keeping fat. Add shallots and thyme. Sauté for 30 seconds. Add fresh corn, salt and pepper. Sauté for one minute, then set aside on paper towel to cool and dry. Once corn is cooked, add potatoes and cheese to corn mixture.

Make Custard:
Mix together. Add custard mixture to corn mixture, a little at a time, until it reaches a somewhat soupy consistency. Place mixture into molds and bake at 350°f for about 20 minutes or until golden brown. Remove from oven. Let stand until cool, remove from mold. Once custard is out of mold, reheat it in over at 350°f for 5-8 minutes.

Blood Orange Salad

Orange

WITH A BRAISED BELGIAN ENDIVE, CANDIED HAZELNUTS,
MAYTAG BLEU CHEESE WITH A DRIED FRUIT VINAIGRETTE,
PAIRED WITH RÉMY VSOP

METHOD

To Braise Endive: Place on stove. Add olive oil and heat. Place endive flat size down and sear endive until golden brown. Turn over and repeat. Add white wine and reduce; season one more time. Pour in orange juice, place in 350°f oven for 1½ hours. Cover pan with foil before placing in over. When done, remove and let cool in own liquid. When cool, chop into ½-inch pieces and separate into 6 portions. Reheat when ready in 350°f for 5 minutes. Serve hot.

Dried Fruit Vinaigrette: *You may substitute your favorite fruit.* In a saucepan, add olive oil and heat. Add sliced shallot and thyme, sauté for one minute over high heat. Season with salt and pepper. Add dried fruit, sauté for 30 seconds. Pour in port wine and cranberry juice, simmer for 30 minutes, seasoning as you go. Set aside and cool. Add mixture to blender and puree. Slowly add vinegar and oil to blender. Once pureed, strain through china cap and taste for seasoning. Refrigerate.

Maytag Bleu Cheese: In a heavy sauté pan, caramelize sugar with cayenne. (Sugar can burn very quickly). Pre-warm hazelnuts in oven at 350°f for 5 minutes. Once sugar is caramelized to light brown, toss in warm hazelnuts and cook for a minute until sugar mixture becomes little darker. Pour onto grated pan rack with second pan underneath. Let cool, then break apart.

Assembly: Reheat endive. Arrange orange segments in a circle around center of plate. Place cheese in center or oranges and pepper cheese. Place small amount of dressing on cheese. Arrange hazelnuts on cheese and around plate. Place hot endive mix on top of cheese. Toss choice of greens (cut small) with salad dressing, salt and pepper. Place on top of endive and serve.

INGREDIENTS

To Braise Endive:
6 Endives, Cut in half and
Seasoned with Salt and Pepper
Medium Size Braising Pan
3 Tbsp. Olive Oil
1 Cup White Wine
3 Cups Orange Juice
Aluminum Foil

Dried Fruit Vinaigrette
½ Cup Dried Cherries*
½ Cup Dried Cranberries*
2 Sprigs Thyme
2 Shallots, Sliced
2 Tbsp. Olive Oil
1 Cup Ruby Red Port
¼ Cup Champagne Vinegar
Or To Taste
¼ Cup Grape Seed Oil
1 Cup Cranberry Juice
Salt and Pepper
2 Quart Saucepan
China Pan/Fine Net
High-Speed Blender

Maytag Bleu Cheese
6 oz. total – 1 oz. per guest
Candied brittle Hazelnuts
1 Cup Sugar
1 Cup Peeled Hazelnuts
1 Pinch Cayenne Pepper

Chef Helene An

CRUSTACEAN

Los Angeles

About the Chef...

The An Family story is that of a family who lived a true "fairy tale life", whose "happily ever after" ending was rudely interrupted by the horrors of the Vietnam War. Executive Chef, **Helene An**, matriarch of the An Family is a "true princess." The great-granddaughter of the Vice-King of Vietnam, young Helene spent all her time in the kitchen with her family's three chefs: Chinese, French and Vietnamese. This later influenced her as she developed her own personal culinary philosophy. Helene's culinary reputation soon took hold. Food critics were quick to recognize *Thanh Long* as being the very first Vietnamese "eatery" in San Francisco, and Chef Helene, as a major force in the culinary world.

Enchanted and inspired by their heritage, the family decided that the next flagship restaurant, Crustacean, in Beverly Hills (1997), would not just be another restaurant, but a celebration of their heritage and culture. *"...When you enter, something magical happens, this is our wish. It is a tribute to our family, my mother's extraordinary childhood in French Colonial Vietnam – a time of refinement and civility,"* says daughter, Elizabeth An.

About the Restaurant...

"Climb every mountain, ford every stream, follow every rainbow, 'til you find your dream."

With kind acknowledgments to the *Sound of Music*, the An Dynasty has come full circle. In a story that evolved just before the fall of Saigon in San Francisco in 1971, with the smash hit success of *Thanh Long*, their American Dream was finally realized in 1991 with the opening of *Crustacean* in San Francisco and finally this, their flagship, **Crustacean**, Beverly Hills in 1997.

The secret to its worldwide recognition is quite simply Helene's resolve to maintain the mysteries of her "secret kitchen". This is an area kept entirely separate from the rest of the restaurant and one where only the family has access. It is here that all the unique flavors are created and shaped from recipes that have been handed down from generation to generation and ultimately treating guests to the supremely sublime menu that is so intrinsically Crustacean.

An eclectic fusing of French, Chinese and Vietnamese influences are apparent in such original starters (or Asian *Tapas*) as Fresh Salmon seared and wrapped in crispy filo, with a chili soy dipping sauce. Equally tantalizing are light puff pastries filled with Dungeness Crab and Comte Francais, accompanied with a peanut mustard emulsion.

No meal at Crustacean is complete without sampling the Lite Vegetarian Series menu- a direct influence of the founder's training in Asian herbal medicine- and one, which promotes "health and well-being" Our choices were the Pacific Rim Style Dumplings consisting of minced mushrooms, carrots, bamboo shoots and water chestnuts, and the Ragout of Fresh Eggplant, Italian pear tomatoes with tofu, tossed with Vietnamese herb "Tia-to". These were not only enjoyable to the palate, but also appealing to the eye, especially the latter in its earthenware crock. Our experience had become a veritable feast fit for an emperor.

Fresh Shrimp Roll

PAIRED WITH RÉMY XO EXCELLENCE

INGREDIENTS

Fresh Shrimp Roll
8 Leaves Green Leaf
Lettuce, Cleaned And Hard
Parts Removed
1 Cup Pickled Carrots*
1/2 Bunch Mint Leaves,
Cleaned And Stems
Removed
1/2 Bunch Chives
2 Cups Cooked Rice
Noodles, Cooled
32 Medium Sized Shrimp,
Boiled, Shelled and
De-Veined.
8 Circular (12" Diameter)
Rice Paper Wrappers
9 White Lint Free Kitchen
Towels, Approximately 13"
Square

*Available at Whole Foods
and Bristol Farms Markets*
Yield: 8 Shrimp rolls

Dipping Sauce:
"Secret Kitchen"
* Sweet Chili Bean Sauce
Or to make your own:
1 Cup Bean Sauce**
1/4 Cup Chardonnay
1/4 Cup Water (optional,
if sauce is too thick for
your taste)
2 Tsp. Sugar
1 Drop Olive oil
1/2 Tsp. Chili
Ground Peanuts to taste

**Bean sauce is available at
Asian Specialty Food Stores.*

METHOD

Prepare rice paper wrappers. Lightly dampen 1 cloth, lay flat and place one rice paper wrapper flat on it. Cover with another damp cloth and place another rice paper on it, alternating layers until all wrappers are done. Flip over the stack and remove towel carefully. Work from bottom of the stack. Place a lettuce leaf 1 inch from the edge of the rice paper, making sure to leave at least 1 inch on all sides to fold. On top of lettuce leaf. Layer rice noodles, pickled carrots, 2 mint leaves, 2 cilantro leaves, 1 chive and 4 shrimps. Vary the amount of each component to taste. Fold top and bottom edges of wrapper toward center of lettuce, forming a rectangular form. Place the 4 shrimp approximately midway between lettuce layer and right edge of the paper. Gently begin rolling whole assembly tightly from left to right enclosing the shrimp last. Set aside and continue assembling rolls until complete. Cut roll in half, then slice each one again. Rolls are best served immediately but will remain fresh for a couple of hours if they are wrapped tightly in plastic and kept at room temperature. Serve with the bean sauce in small dipping bowls.

Drunken Crab

PAIRED WITH RÉMY VSOP

METHOD

Drunken Crab:

Scrub crab with a stiff brush under cold running water until white and smooth. Turn crab over on its shell and with a kitchen knife cut in half and then in quarters. Place crab pieces in a clean skillet or pan. Pour in fish broth, fish sauce, ginger and garlic. Cover pan and bring to boil for 3 minutes. Add Chardonnay, green onions, black pepper and sugar. Cover and let boil 5 to 7 minutes.

Serving:

Take out cooked crab pieces and place on a warm serving platter. Pour sauce over crab. Garnish with cilantro and scallion and serve.

INGREDIENTS

Drunken Crab

1 Of 2-2½ lbs. Fresh Crab	*Cooking Wine or Sake*
1 Cup Fish Broth	½ Cup Green Onion
1 Tsp. Nuoc Mam*	½ Tsp. Black Pepper
(Vietnamese Fish Sauce)	½ Tsp. Sugar
3 Slices Fresh Ginger	Cilantro and Scallions to
1 Tsp. Chopped Garlic	Garnish
¼ Cup Chardonnay or	*Available in Asian Markets*

INGREDIENTS

Roasted Filet Mignon

3 Lbs. Beef Bone	8 Bay Leaves
(Neck Bone)	1 Fennel Root
1 Filet Mignon	¼ Tsp. Black Pepper
5 Onions	1 Tsp. Salt
2 oz. Ginger	¼ Tsp. Garlic Powder
½ Bunch Parsley	6 Cloves Garlic
4 Carrots	¼ Cup Vegetable Oil

Roasted Filet Mignon

PAIRED WITH RÉMY LOUIS XIII

METHOD

Beef Broth:

Put bone in the pot; bring to boil about 5 to 10 minutes. Rinse with warm water until water runs clear, then put back in pot, fill up with 8 cups of warm water, then add 2 onions (grilled), ¼ teaspoon salt and ginger. Simmer on low heat for one hour until liquid yields approximately 5 cups of broth. Sauté 2 onions (sliced); add ½ bunch of parsley, root of fennel (sliced), 4 carrots (sliced) and 4 bay leaves. Then add sautéed ingredients to beef broth, reduce and simmer until liquid yields 2 cups of sauce.

Mash 6 cloves of garlic, massage over the filet. Marinate filet in mixture of ¼ tsp garlic powder, ¼ tsp black pepper, 1 tsp salt and ¼ cup vegetable oil for one hour. Heat sauté pan on high heat with one tsp oil. Preheat oven for 10 minutes. When sauté pan is hot, put filet in pan and sear until golden brown. Remove filet from sauté pan. Place one sliced onion in roasting pan, then place filet on top of onion. Pour two cups of sauce over filet, place four bay leaves on top of filet, then roast filet at 350°f for 30 minutes.

Serving:

Suggested accompaniments would be grilled zucchini, eggplant, carrots, asparagus tip.

Proceed to place zucchini in the center of serving platter, surrounded by carrots, asparagus and eggplant with filet on top. Finish by pouring sauce over filet.

Chef Suzanne Goin

About the chef...

Graduating from Brown University in 1988, **Suzanne Goin** had already worked at top restaurants such as Providence's *Al Forno*, London's *Le Mazarin*, and Los Angeles' *Ma Maison* and *L'Orangerie*.

She then cooked at *Chez Panisse* before moving to France, where she developed her talents working at Didier Oudill's two-star restaurant *Pain, Adour Et Fantasie*, Alain Passard's three-starred *Arpege* and *Patisserie Christian Pottier* in Paris.

In 1994 Suzanne left for *Alloro*, in Boston, being named "Best Creative Chef" by *Boston Magazine* in August. Upon returning to Los Angeles in 1995, Suzanne spent two years at *Campanile*. In September 1998, she opened *Lucques*, in the former carriage house of film actor Harold Lloyd.

Her credits include 1999 *Food & Wine's* "Best New Chefs of 1999." 1999 – *Condé Nast Traveler* –"50 Hot Tables – the World's Most Exciting Restaurants", Gourmet – one of the "top six restaurants in Los Angeles" (2000) *Bon Appetit*- " favorite restaurants" (2000)

About the Restaurant...

Continuing to astonish the discriminating Beverly Hills set and Hollywood foodies alike, Suzanne Goin is indeed a remarkable chef. Enclosed by a "restaurant row" of predominately male chef proprietors, Chef Goin, with her adventurous approach to modern cuisine, cannot it seems do any wrong with, either, the national press or that most critical of food pundits, LA Times' Irene Verbilas!

Since the highly publicized opening a year or so ago, fashionable **Lucques**, with its tranquil unhurried ambiance, has become a firmly established member of California's elite 5-star restaurants. Its design, a combination of modern American with hi-tech Italian accents and cool shades of gray, provide a contrepoint to the warmth and vibrancy of the open fireplace that greets you upon entering.

Deceptively spacious, the restaurant offers seating in the open-plan bar/lounge/dining room, or in the rear conservatory, which provides a bright airy oasis in summer and a cozy retreat in winter.

Using only organic ingredients, Goin's lunch and dinner seasonal menus ambitiously reflect a fusing of French, Californian, and middle-eastern influences, living up to high expectations. The Parsnip soup with fried parsnips, black mustard and yogurt, the Spiced Snapper with carrot puree, chickpea fritters and gingered beet chutney, and the irresistible veal chop with spring onion soubise, cavolo nero, crisp prosciutto and truffle butter, are all exceptional choices.

Her limited dessert menu is very much a "quality rather than quantity" statement. When we dined she offered the Coconut Cake wrapped in filo, with peaches and blackberries, and the Espresso Meringues with ice creams and caramel mousse – both highly recommended.

There also is devotion to a serious wine list. This offers quality champagnes from the smaller houses, and a selection of top-notch red and white varieties from the French regions, Europe and California, with an enterprising section labeled "Elsewhere."

Go girl!

Layered Brique

WITH WALNUTS, PISTACHIOS, HONEY AND YOGURT SORBET.
PAIRED WITH RÉMY VSOP

INGREDIENTS

8 Pieces Brique Pastry
1¾ Cup Lightly Toasted Walnuts
½ Cup Coarsely Chopped Pistachios
2 Tbsp. Finely Chopped Pistachios
½ Cup Sugar
½ Cup Brown Sugar
½ Teaspoon Freshly Grated Nutmeg
¼ Cup + 2 Tablespoons Clarified Unsalted Butter, Lightly Browned
1 Tablespoon Honey
1 Teaspoon Fleur De Sel
*One recipe hazelnut brittle
**One recipe yogurt sorbet
Serves 8

Hazelnut brittle*
2 Cups Sugar
1 Tbsp. Corn Syrup
2 Cups Toasted Hazelnuts
3 Tbsp. Unsalted Butter
Makes one half sheet pan

Yogurt sorbet**
¼ Cup Water
1½ Tbsp. Sugar
2 Tbsp. Corn Syrup
2 Cups Whole Milk Yogurt
¾ Cup Crème Fraîche
½ Cup Cream
1 Tsp. Lemon Juice
Makes 1 quart

METHOD

Preheat oven to 350°f.

Combine both sugars and walnuts in food processor and process until mixture is well combined and a medium grind. Fold coarsely chopped pistachios into walnut mixture. Add nutmeg and ¼ cup of butter and mix until incorporated. Place one piece of brique on a sheet pan lined with parchment paper. Brush a little butter on pastry and place another piece of brique on top. Evenly spread ⅓ of filling over pastry with your hands. Continue with two more buttered pastry layers and so on until you have 3 layers of filling. Finish with two layers of brique and brush top with butter. Bake for 15-20 minutes until top is golden brown. To assemble cut brique into 8 wedges and place each piece off-center on a plate. Break 8x2" pieces and 8x3" pieces of brittle from the large piece. On each plate place 2" and a 3" piece of brittle next to wedge of brique. The brittle will serve as an anchor for the sorbet. Sprinkle small pinch of fleur de sel over brittle. Scoop yogurt sorbet and place it on the brittle—make sure you can still see the brittle. Sprinkle finely chopped pistachios all over dessert. Warm honey in a jar over hot water and drizzle it over the plate. Serve immediately.

Hazelnut brittle*

Butter ½ sheet pan. Bring sugar, corn syrup and ¼ cup water to medium caramel (brushing down sides often with a pastry brush and cold water.) Add hazelnuts to caramel. Mix and add butter. Mix constantly until well incorporated. Using an offset spatula, spread mixture as thin as possible on prepared sheet pan. Place sheet pan in freezer to set. Break brittle into desired size pieces and store in an airtight container.

Yogurt sorbet**

Combine water and sugar in small pot. Bring to boil, making sure sugar dissolves. Set aside to cool. Combine all ingredients (except for sugar syrup). Whisk until smooth. Whisk in simple syrup. Freeze according to ice cream machine instructions.

Duck Confit

WITH YOUNG TURNIPS AND CANDIED KUMQUATS.
PAIRED WITH RÉMY 1738

METHOD

Clean duck legs and leave out at room temperature for 30 minutes. Season with salt, pepper and 1½ tbsp thyme leaves and let them sit out for another 30 minutes in a roasting or braising dish that will just hold the duck legs. Scatter orange slices, thyme springs and star anise. Place duck legs in dish skin side up. Pour duck fat over until it almost covers duck. Cook duck legs in a 300°f oven for 3 hours or until tender. When duck is tender pour off some of the fat, turn oven up to 400° and let duck skin crisp. While duck is in oven, bring water and sugar to boil in saucepot. When sugar is dissolved add kumquats and cheesecloth bundle. Reduce heat to a simmer, cover top surface of the liquid with piece of parchment paper and rest a small plate on top to ensure kumquats are submerged in liquid.

After 30 minutes check kumquats. Continue cooking until translucent and flesh inside next to the seeds is jelly-like. Meanwhile, thinly slice turnips lengthwise leaving tops intact. Clean and dry turnip tops. Slice spring onions into thin wedges. Julienne spring onion tops on the bias. When duck is ready, gently sauté spring onions in 2 tbsp butter with ½ tbsp thyme leaves until just translucent. Add turnips, let them wilt and quickly add greens and onion tops. Season with salt and pepper to taste. Immediately plate vegetables in a natural style. Strain duck from the fat and place on top of turnips. Bring sauce to boil. Spoon 1 tbsp butter over duck. Finally spoon warmed kumquats over duck and serve immediately.

INGREDIENTS

Duck Confit
6 Large Duck Legs
2 Tablespoons Fresh Thyme
Leaves Plus ½ Bunch
Thyme
Duck Fat to Cover
(Approximately 6 Cups)
3 Star Anise
2 Oranges, Thickly Sliced
2 Bunches Young Turnips
6 Small Spring Onions with
Tops
¾ Cup Duck Sauce Made
From Roasted Carcasses,
White Wine and Mirepoix
3 Tablespoons Unsalted Butter
1 Cup Kumquats
3 Cups Sugar
3 Cups Water
Small Handful White
Peppercorns, Bay Leaf and A
Dried Chili Tied In
Cheesecloth
Serves 6

Chef Celestino Drago

DRAGO

About the Chef...

Celestino Drago was born and raised in the bucolic farm country of Galati Mamartino in northern Sicily overlooking the Aeolian Islands. His family raised and made almost everything it ate. It is an appreciation for superior ingredients that suffuses his professional life.

Whilst at a design school in Pisa, for spending money, he worked at a local restaurant as a bus boy. There, he caught the eye of Chef Ignazio Diana – as a result, he went to work full time in the kitchen. He became a voracious reader of cookbooks, especially those of master chef Paul Bocuse and began challenging himself to create elegant new dishes.

In the last sixteen years, the Drago name has become synonymous with the evolution of modern Italian cooking.

About the Restaurant...

Drago hails from Sicily – and my, how it shows! The flagship of a small group, *Drago* makes a statement of loving tribute to all that is the quintessential best in Sicilian Cucina.

During lunch, the restaurant provides the perfect languorous oasis in the busy thoroughfare of Santa Monica. At night it becomes a buzzing affair. The stark white walls, crisp white napery and contrasting sea-foam green dining chairs, along with softly underscored background music, complete the perfect ambiance in which to experience stellar gourmet cuisine at its pinnacle best.

A well-informed staff is proud to carry Chef Drago's unique presentations to your table. The seduction begins by your indulgence in his antipasti. Among them are the Insalata Primavera (a salad of baby lettuces, grilled eggplant, roasted bell peppers and goat cheese) or the Timbale di Melanzane ai Sapori Isolani (eggplant soufflé with tomato and basil sauce).

The grand cantata continues with the Drago signatures of Tortellini Di Zucca al Burro e Salvia (pumpkin tortelloni with butter and sage sauce) and Costolette d'Agnello con Cus-cus e Salsa D'Aglio Arrosto (oven-roasted rack of lamb with giant cous-cous and roasted garlic sauce). Both are unique and exceptional (the key lies in Celestino's ability to blend flavours to achieve taste and balance).

Complement your meal with a choice from the wine list – a vivid illustration of spot-on pairing with the quality and variety of Drago's menu. Much emphasis is naturally on Italian reds, especially a Brunello di Montalcino col d'Orcia, 1988.

But it is the final passage in this finely orchestrated dining experience that supplies you with an exciting breathtaking surge before curtain down and that is the dazzling array of dolci, including a signature classic Tirasmisu cone-all sweetness and light, as is a mouthwatering Panacotti in a fresh strawberry cone.

Celestino – *Veni Vedi Vici* – indeed!

Los Angeles

Roasted Rack of Lamb

WITH THYME, SERVED WITH 25 YEAR OLD BALSAMIC VINEGAR
AND EXTRA VIRGIN OLIVE OIL. PAIRED WITH RÉMY XO EXCELLENCE

METHOD

Roasted Rack of Lamb

In a sauté pan add olive oil; heat until oil is very hot. Season lamb with thyme, salt & pepper and evenly sear on both sides. Place lamb in a pre heated 450°f oven for about 10-15 minutes for medium rare. Remove from oven and let rest in warm place for about 5 minutes. Cut rack into chops; place on a plate with your favorite grilled vegetables or potato. Drizzle balsamic vinegar and olive oil on top and serve.

INGREDIENTS

Roasted Rack of Lamb
1 Colorado Lamb Rack
1 Tbsp. Chopped Fresh Thyme
Sea Salt and Fresh Ground Pepper
2 Tbsp. Olive Oil For Sautéing
2 Tbsp. 25 Years Old Balsamic Vinegar
2 Tbsp. Extra Virgin Olive Oil

Bigoli con Scampi e Pepe Verde

BIGOLI PASTA WITH LANGOSTINO AND GREEN PEPPERCORN. PAIRED WITH RÉMY VSOP

Bigoli Pasta with Langostino and Green Peppercorn:

In a large sauté pan add olive oil, shallots, garlic and green peppercorn. Sauté until golden color; add langostinos and let cook for about 2 minutes. Add salt & pepper, white wine and brandy. Let evaporate for about 2-3 minutes. Add tomato puree and chopped tomatoes. Cook for about 5 minutes or until sauce is semi-thick. Remove from flame and set aside. In a large pot of boiling salted water cook Bigoli *al dente*. Drain and add to sauce and toss well. Add chopped Italian parsley and serve.

Bigoli Pasta with Langostino and Green Peppercorn	1/2 Tbsp. Chopped Garlic
1 lb. Bigoli Pasta or Homemade Fresh Thick Spaghetti	1 Tbsp. Green Peppercorn in Brine
	1/4 Cup Olive Oil
	1 Cup Tomato Puree
12 Med. Langostino – Cut Lengthwise	1/2 Cup Chopped Tomato
	Salt & Pepper To Taste
1 Tbsp. Chopped Shallots	1/4 Cup Dry White Wine
	2 Tbsp. Brandy

Tiramisu

6 Egg Yolks	2 Cup Strong Espresso Coffee
6 oz. Sugar	
2 Tsp. Vanilla Extract	2 Cup Packages of Lady Fingers
8 oz. Mascarpone Cheese	
1 Cup Manufacturing Cream	2 Tsp. Cocoa Powder For Dusting

Tiramisu

PAIRED WITH RÉMY 1738

Tiramisu

In a mixing bowl, add yolks, sugar, and vanilla. Beat until foaming. Add mascarpone and beat until creamy and smooth. Whip cream to soft peaks. Carefully fold whipped cream into egg yolk mixture. Cover and refrigerate for 10 to 15 minutes. Place espresso in shallow bowl and quickly dip lady fingers into espresso. Place lady fingers on towel lined baking sheets to absorb excess espresso. Using individual molds or a 3" deep baking dish (for self- serve dessert buffets) spread a layer of cream mixture on the bottom of mold, then the espresso dipped lady fingers. Repeat this until you reach top of the mold making sure you smooth cream mixture with a spatula. Refrigerate for 2 hours.

Dust with cocoa powder just before serving. Serve with vanilla or chocolate sauce.

Chef Mark Militello

About the Chef...

Chef *Mark Militello*, who has been credited with putting South Florida on America's culinary map in the late '80s and early '90s, sent shock waves through the Florida dining community in 1994, with the opening of *Mark's Las Olas* in Fort Lauderdale.

Since then and with a further opening, *Mark's South Beach*, Militello's seemingly effortless innovative contemporary American cuisine, combined with the restaurant's sophisticated design and top-notch service, has placed both establishments in the crème de la crème of South Florida's top dining destinations, with marked appreciation from the pundits. A steady stream of top awards, including a James Beard Award for Best Regional Chef and *Food & Wine* magazine's "Best Restaurant Award" have helped cement Militello's reputation as one of the most creative and successful chefs in the country.

Both venues, which defined hip, cutting edge cuisine upon opening, remain fresh and inspired "many moons" later.

About the Restaurant...

South Beach oozes sex appeal, from the flashy cars that cruise the streets to the beautiful people who walk them. Mingling here in this city requires the perfect blend of sleek sophistication and a savvy attitude. A cocktail here, a cigar there, and a stroll down the warm deco-dreamy street will build an appetite for *The Great Gatsby*- style of **Mark's South Beach.**

Located inside the art deco-inspired Hotel Nash, where the lobby bleeds into the mahogany and gold restaurant – much like Hollywood's star- studded Standard Hotel, Mark's' is most certainly the place to be and be seen. Serving a perfectly presented Mediterranean/American cuisine, that is predominantly

seafood, owner Mark Militello and executive Chef Tim Andriola have captured in their items, the concept that less is most definitely more. The Yellow fin Tuna Carpaccio, for example, served with hearts of palm, citrus and black pepper is an elegant choice – delicate yet flavorful, this perfect pairing of ingredients is both healthy and light. As an entrée, the Vegetable-wrapped Maine Lobster and Veal Tenderloin with apple-wood smoked bacon and olive oil Béarnaise sauce is an innovative variation of the classic surf and turf specialty. Both dishes encompass Militello's and Andriola's attempts to create a refined world-class menu in a hip and happening environment.

Guests can dine on the terrace next to one of this historic hotel's three pools, fresh water, mineral, or salt water. It's a choice spot to indulge in one of pastry chef Juan Villaparedes' decadent desserts. A personal favorite is the Coffee Crème Brûlée Napoleon with caramelized bananas, vanilla orange syrup and espresso drizzle.

Super-suave, super-sharp, and sumptuously delicious, Mark's has become a welcoming home for an eclectic crowd of trendsetters, devout gourmets, and celebs alike. And Militello has certainly paved the way for chic yet serious restaurants in South Beach.

Peppered Tenderloin of Veal

WITH CHANTERELLES AND COGNAC. PAIRED WITH RÉMY 1738

INGREDIENTS

**Peppered Tenderloin
of Veal**
6 5 oz. Veal Butt Tenderloin
Portions
Sea Salt and Freshly Ground
Pepper
1/4 Cup Chopped Fresh Herbs,
Such As Sage, Basil, Parsley
And Thyme
12 Paper Thin Slices of
Prosciutto
2 Tbsp. Cracked Peppercorns
Clarified Butter or Pure Olive
Oil
6 Cups Fresh Wild
Mushrooms, Such As
Chanterelles
1/3 Cup Shallots, Minces
3/4 Cup Cognac
3 Cups Light Brown
Veal Stock
1/3 Cup Cold Butter, Cut Into
Small Pieces

Serves 6
Creamy Gorgonzola Polenta
6 1/4 Cups Water
1 Tbsp. Sea Salt
1 Tbsp. Olive Oil
1 1/2 Cups Quick Cooking
Polenta
3/4 Cup Parmesan Cheese,
Grated
3/4 Cup Heavy Cream
1 Cup Gorgonzola Cheese,
Crumbled

METHOD

Peppered Tenderloin of Veal

Preheat oven to 375°f. Season veal with salt and pepper. Spread chopped herbs on a cutting board and roll veal in them. For each portion of veal, lay two slices of prosciutto end-to-end, overlapping slightly. Envelop veal by rolling it in prosciutto. Spread cracked peppercorns on cutting board and roll prosciutto-wrapped veal in them pressing firmly. In large sauté pan over medium heat, heat clarified butter or pure olive oil to almost smoking. Sear veal portions on all sides; transfer to baking sheet. Place in oven for about 7 minutes. Meanwhile, discard about half the fat from sauté pan. Sauté mushrooms until lightly browned. Add shallots, stir, continue to cook about 2 minutes. Deglaze pan with cognac, reduce by half. Add veal stock; simmer over high heat, reducing sauce until it is of a nappe consistency. Whisk in cold butter, one bit at a time until all incorporated. Adjust seasoning. When veal is cooked to desired doneness, remove from oven, cover loosely with foil, keep warm.

Creamy Gorgonzola Polenta

Bring water, salt and olive oil to boil. Remove from heat and vigorously whisk in all polenta. Replace on heat and lower to medium heat, stirring constantly for 5-6 minutes. Turn off heat. Fold in Parmesan cheese, cream and Gorgonzola cheese. Adjust seasoning and consistency (with water or cream) if necessary.

Coffee Cognac Crème Brûlée Napoleon

WITH CARAMELIZED BANANAS, STRAWBERRIES, AND ESPRESSO DRIZZLE.
PAIRED WITH RÉMY VSOP (CHILLED)

METHOD

For the Crème Brûlée: Preheat oven to 300°f. Using a paring knife, split vanilla bean down middle lengthwise, scrape beans out of pod. Add both beans and pod to cream in a heavy non-reactive saucepan. Bring to boil. Turn off heat and allow to steep for about 10 minutes. Combine yolks with sugar in stainless steel bowl, whisk vigorously until mixture turns pale yellow. In small amounts, slowly incorporate hot cream into yolks, whisking continuously. Stir in coffee granules and Rémy Martin XO Excellence. Strain custard through fine mesh sieve. Chill over an ice water bath. Pour cooled mixture into four 6-oz. ramekins and place them into a water bath. Cover water bath with aluminum foil. Bake for approx. 25-30 minutes. When done they will be firm along edges but should jiggle towards center. Remove from water bath. Refrigerate 4-6 hours before assembling.

For the Pastry: Preheat over to 350°f. Cover a baking sheet with parchment paper. Cut 12 pieces puff pastry using 3" round cutter, arrange evenly on baking sheet. Place another piece of parchment paper on top of pastry, then another baking sheet on top of paper. Bake for 15-20 minutes until golden brown, light and flaky. Can be stored in airtight container for up to 3 days.

For the Strawberries: Dice berries and place in stainless steel bowl. In another stainless steel bowl, combine sugar, orange zest and vanilla bean specks. Muddle mixture and sprinkle it over berries, tossing them. Cover and store in refrigerator.

For Espresso drizzle: Mix reduced espresso & honey; reserve for garnish of plate.

For Caramelized Bananas: Using small round scooper, scoop out 12 banana balls, toss in sugar. On baking sheet caramelize them with blowtorch until golden brown. Should be right before assembly.

For Optional sugar ring garnish: Dissolve water into sugar in small saucepot, add squeeze of lemon and transfer to high heat. When sugar has dissolved, add glucose. Boil until sugar has reached light amber color. Remove from heat and allow to cool for 5 minutes. With a small spoon, spread sugar in an eight inch strip on a Silpat Mat, moving your hand back and forth quickly, not lettering sugar bead up. Moving quickly, pull off sugar strip and wrap it around a small ring mold or round metal object (aluminum can) forming sugar ring. These can be stored up to 2 days in airtight container.

Assembly: Arrange 3 bananas in circle at bottom, leaving room in center for dollop of brûlèe. Brûlèe can be spooned out and leveled. Top with one circle puff pastry, one tbsp strawberries, more brûlèe. Repeat layers twice more. Place sugar ring garnish atop and drizzle espresso syrup on the plate.

INGREDIENTS

For The Brûlèe
2 Cups Heavy Cream
6 Large Egg Yolks
1/2 Cup Sugar
1 Tsp. Instant Coffee Granules
1 Tbsp. Rémy Martin XO Excellence
1 Vanilla Bean
(Or 1 Tbsp Vanilla Extract)

For The Pastry
1 Sheet Frozen Puff Pasty

For The Strawberries
12 Strawberries Cleaned And Hulled
Zest Of One Orange
1/4 Cup Sugar
1 Vanilla Bean, Scraped

For The Espresso Drizzle
1/2 Cup Espresso Reduced To One Tablespoon
1 Tbsp. Honey

For The Caramelized Bananas
2 Bananas
3-4 Tbsp. Sugar

For The Optional Sugar Garnish
6 oz. Sugar
1 oz. Water
Squeeze Of Lemon
1 oz. Glucose or Corn Syrup
Serves 4

Chef Norman Van Aken

About the Chef...

Norman Van Aken is internationally reputed for his innovative New World Cuisine, and has been recognized by the *New York Times* as "South Florida's Most Gifted Chef." His career reads like a "Who's who", with such recognition as *TIME magazine, The Wine Spectator, Newsweek, CNN, Good Morning America, TVFN,* and *Discovery Channel,* including *Condé Nast Traveler* naming Norman's as "one of the Top Ten restaurants in the U.S."

He has received the Ivy Award, James Beard Award, the Robert Mondavi Award and the Food Arts Silver Spoon Award for lifetime achievements. Not surprisingly he has been named one of the top 25 people who mattered the most in the history of South Florida by the *St. Petersburg Times.* In addition to being one of America's Top Chefs, with three cookbooks published and a fourth on the way, Norman Van Aken is also highly regarded as an author.

About the Restaurant...

"Tell me what you eat, and I shall tell you what you are" – French Gastronomer **Jean-Anthelme Brillat-Savarin.**

Established as Florida's "Most outstanding restaurant," *Norman's* is your voyage to a "Brave New World" of shapes, colors and scents. Like the designer of the richest of tapestries, Van Aken is the master weaver, as he fashions a profusion of spices and ingredients. The result reveals his internationally acclaimed "New World Cuisine." He dares to fuse styles to complement his unique recipes, resulting in dishes of passion and depth served in the dramatic kitchen-dining room.

Our personal choices for starters were Peeky Toe Crab Salad stuffed Brazilian black eyed pea Acaraje with sun dried tomato and avocado Salsita. Ever the traditionalist, I also opted for the refreshing, no-nonsense and unadorned Classic Caesar Salad with hard cooked eggs, tomatoes and steak tartare.

At main course stage, we were treated to a masterful demonstration with such revolutionary revelations as Cooked Fillet of Key West Yellowtail on a belly of mashed potatoes with grilled asparagus spears and citrus butter and Chef Norman's majestic Roasted Pork "Havana" with "21st Century" Mole, and Black Bean Salsa.

The final *denouement,* comes from his "just released" repertoire, where he follows his heart with an enticing rendition of a classic "Peaches & Cream". And taking our "trip on his magic swirling ship" *(thanks, Bob!)* we also indulged in his Caramelized Apple Turnovers with pecan brittle, rosemary caramel and vanilla ice cream and banana chips-which guaranteed to tantalize all our senses!

If you are in a really indulgent mood, then try the cheese board with some vintage port or Madeira. It offers a selection unrivaled by many current illustrious restaurants- we counted at least eighteen varieties from Europe, and seven from the USA.

Norman's Caramelized Apple Turnovers

WITH PECAN BRITTLE, ROSEMARY CARAMEL AND VANILLA ICE CREAM. PAIRED WITH RÉMY VSOP

INGREDIENTS

For the Rosemary caramel:
7 oz. Sugar
Apple Juice as Needed
1 Rosemary Sprig
8 oz. Heavy Cream
1 Tsp. Vanilla Extract
Boil sugar & apple juice with sprig to a caramel. Whisk in cream and vanilla.

For the apple filling:
1 Vanilla Bean
1/3 Cup Granulated Sugar
6 Granny Smith Apples, Peeled, Cored and Sliced Thin
2 oz. Butter
1 Cup Applejack

For The Puff Pastry:
You can use your favorite recipe or buy from your local grocery store.

For The Pecan Brittle:
1 Cup Sugar
8 oz. Corn Syrup
1/4 Tsp. Salt
3/4 Tsp. Baking Soda
1 Tbsp. Butter
2 Cups Toasted Pecans
1 Tsp. Vanilla

METHOD

For the Rosemary caramel: Boil sugar & apple juice with sprig to a caramel. Whisk in cream and vanilla.

For the apple filling: Split the vanilla bean lengthwise with sharp knife. Sprinkle sugar over bean scrape seeds out of bean and rub into sugar. This will separate the vanilla bean seeds into sugar. Toss apples with vanilla bean sugar. In a large non-stick skillet melt butter, over medium heat, and sauté apples, stirring gently occasionally until they are soft. Deglaze skillet with applejack, being very careful because it may ignite to burn off the alcohol. Continue to sauté about another minute and remove skillet from heat.

For The Puff Pastry: You can use your favorite recipe or buy from your local grocery store.

For The Pecan Brittle: Boil sugar and corn syrup to a caramel. Add butter, salt, vanilla, baking soda. Mix thoroughly. Add nuts. Pour onto a baking sheet to cool.

To assemble: Cut puff pastry in squares. Add filling in middle and fold it corner to corner using some water to seal inside edges. Brush with eggwash and sprinkle with coarse granulated natural sugar. Bake at 385°f for 19 minutes.

To make dish: Drizzle turnovers with caramel and top with brittle. Serve your favorite vanilla ice cream on the side.

"Down Island" French Toast

WITH A SAVORY-CITRUS CARAMEL. PAIRED WITH RÉMY XO EXCELLENCE

METHOD

For the Foie Gras and the Marinade: Mix liqueur with vanilla bean, scraping out seeds into the liqueur with the tip of a knife. Add mace, cinnamon, orange peel and whisk. Place foie gras into marinade, cover it with plastic wrap and slosh around a bit. Refrigerate until ready to serve. (Allow at least 12 hours in the marinade.)

For the French Toast: Scrape vanilla seeds out of the bean into the beaten eggs. Add half-and-half, mace and cinnamon. Beat a bit more. Now slip slices of brioche into eggs and allow them to flavor. The amount of time in the eggs will vary depending on softness of your brioche. The softer, the shorter. Keep covered and refrigerated until ready to prepare dish.

To make the dish: 1 recipe prepared and heated Savory-Citrus Caramel Sauce (see below). Remove foie gras from marinade and slice into wafer cuts approx. 1/3" thick and reserve on chilled plate. Discard the marinade. Remove brioche from marinade and lay slices onto a plate. Season foie gras with sea salt & fresh cracked black pepper. Heat a skillet like you would use for making classic French toast. Start with the toast by ladling some clarified butter into bottom of it. Add brioche and cook on moderate heat until golden on both sides.. Keep warm in the oven a moment. Add some of the previously warmed caramel to the bottom of 4 hot plates. Now heat a non-stick skillet. When pan is quite hot, sear foie gras on both sides and place on four plates. Drizzle some warm Savory Caramel around the toasts. Serve.

For the Savory Citrus Caramel: Combine stock, passion fruit juice and sugar in heavy but shallow saucepan and cook to the caramel stage. Carefully whisk in heavy cream. Allow to boil, deepen in color and reduce, whisking constantly. When it is caramel dark and reduced to 1-1½ cups add soy sauce and then strain through fine meshed strainer. Reserve.

Candied Lime Zest: Rinse lime zests. Boil in two changes of water. Put zest in small saucepan with ginger, sugar and water. Reduce until liquid is almost all gone. Reserve.

INGREDIENTS

For the Foie Gras and the Marinade
12 oz. of Fresh Foie Gras, Cleaned and Cut into 2 Sections
1 Tahitian Vanilla Bean Cut In Half Length-Wise
1 Cup Of Cointreau or Curacao
1 Tsp. Mace
1 Tsp. Cinnamon
Peel Of One Orange, All Pith Removed
Serves 4

For the French Toast
12 Slices Of Fresh Brioche, Cut 1/3" In Thickness
5 Whole Eggs, Beaten Together
2 Cups Half and Half
1 Tahitian Vanilla Bean Cut In Half Length-Wise
1 Tsp. Mace
1 Tsp. Cinnamon
Some Clarified Butter To Cook The Toast Off In

For the Savory Citrus Caramel:
14 oz. Chicken Stock
1 Cup Passion Fruit
1 Cup Sugar
2 Cups Heavy Cream
A Few Drops of Soy Sauce
Yield 1 to 1½ cups

Candied Lime Zest
Zest of 4 limes
3 inch piece of ginger, peeled and finely julienned
2/3 Cup water
3 Tablespoons sugar

Chef Susan Spicer

BAYONA

About the Chef...

In 1979, **Susan Spicer** became an apprentice at the *Louis XVI* Restaurant in New Orleans. Leaving in 1982, Spicer worked under Roland Durand at the Hotel Sofitel in Paris. Later she became Executive Chef at the *Savoir Faire* in New Orleans.

After opening the *Bistro* at Maison DeVille in New Orleans in 1986, Susan was voted one of Ten Best New Chefs by *Food & Wine* magazine. In 1990, she became the co-owner of *Bayona*, where she received the James Beard Award for Best Chef, Southeast Region in 1993. Since then there have been more accolades including Robert Mondavi Culinary Award of Excellence (1995), the Ivy Award from Restaurants and Institutions Magazine (1996) and *Number One Restaurant* in Gourmet magazine by Readers' Choice Poll America's Top Tables (1996).

Her other enterprises include *Spice, Inc.*, a gourmet retail store and cooking school in the Warehouse District of New Orleans, *Cobalt* at the Monaco and *Herbsaint*, a casual contemporary Bistro-style restaurant.

About the Restaurant...

Craig Claiborne, the venerable former New York Times food critic, raconteur and celebrity chef, naturally as a Southerner, claimed *"N' Owlens"* was "the home of American Cooking," and not without some foundation. This exciting, intriguing, mysterious city has long held an attraction for the adventurous – dining or otherwise.

Blessed with the likes of Paul Prudhomme, Emeril Legasse and Renee Bajeux, the city is now ready to embrace the new development from local talent, James Beard Award recipient for Best

Chef in Southwest Region, Susan Spicer. Gourmets have surely heard the blue buzz about Cobalt housed in the splendidly deco Hotel Monaco, and her diversification with Spice, Inc., a specialty cooking concept and market and Wild Flour Breads. But at *Bayona*, where she has been Executive Chef and co-owner for the last twelve years, Spicer seems particularly at home.

Located in a 200 year-old Creole cottage in the heart of the romantic yet bustling French Quarter, Bayona offers "New Southern" dishes, as Spicer likes to call it – not just Creole or Cajun, just flavorful and vibrant. As a starter, the Sautéed Sweetbreads with potatoes, mushrooms and sherry mustard are a delicious first choice as is the bold Cream of Garlic Soup. Her varied influences are apparent in dishes that range from Grilled Yellowfin Tuna with Israeli cous cous and Lobster sauce, to Kentucky Bibb with Nicoise olives, haricot verts, quail eggs and balsamic vinaigrette.

The same vibrancy seen in her cuisine is evident in both Spicer's personality and the ambiance of her restaurant. In the kitchen she wears a red bandanna, and puts a bright orange crayfish on a plate for decoration or her signature celery leaves – simply to bring a smile or brighten someone's day. In the dining room the terracotta walls give a warm European yet down to earth feel and the beautiful outdoor courtyard is a fresh and elegant place to dine.

Sautéed Sweetbreads

WITH CRAYFISH SAUCE. PAIRED WITH RÉMY XO EXCELLENCE

INGREDIENTS

1 Tbsp. Butter
1 Ea. Onion, Carrot and Celery Stalk, Chopped
1 lb. Veal Sweetbreads, Soaked in Cold Water Overnight
1 Cup White Wine
1 Bay Leaf
Salt and Pepper
Flour For Dusting
2-3 Tbsp. Clarified Butter
Serves 4

For sauce:
2 Tbsp. Butter
1 Cup Onion, Finely Diced
1 Stalk Celery, Finely Diced
1 Small Carrot, Peeled And Diced
1 oz. Pancetta, Cut In Small Dice
1 Garlic Clove, Sliced
1 Cup Chopped Fresh Tomato
1 Cup Madeira
1 Cup White Wine
2 Cups Veal or Dark Chicken Stock
2 Cup Stock Made From Shrimp or Crayfish Shells
Bouquet Garni Of 4 Thyme And 2 Tarragon Stems
(Save Leaves To Finish Sauce)
Softened Butter
Salt and Cayenne Pepper
Lemon Juice

To assemble dish:
1 Tbsp. Butter
1/2 Cup Sliced Mushrooms *(Your Choice)*
1/4 Lb, Fresh Crayfish Tails
1 Tbsp. Mixed Chopped Thyme And Tarragon Sauce
Chopped Chives

METHOD

Melt butter in a 4-qt pot and add onion, carrot and celery. Sweat over medium heat for about 5 minutes, remove sweetbreads from water and place in pot. Add white wine, bay leaf and enough cold water to cover sweetbreads. Bring to boil and reduce heat. Simmer about 6-8 minutes until sweetbreads are firm but not hard. Remove one lobe from pot and plunge into ice water to test for firmness. Place cooked sweetbreads on plate or in a pan, place another plate or pan on top with about a 2lb weight on top of that. Refrigerate until cool; trim outside of excess fat and membrane and cut into thick slices. When ready to serve, light season slices with salt and pepper and dust with flour. Heat clarified butter to almost smoking in a large sauté pan, shake excess flour off slices and sauté for 3-4 minutes, or until golden brown, on both sides. Remove from heat, drain on paper towels and keep warm until ready to sauce.

For sauce:
Heat butter in a 4-qt pot and sauté onion, carrot, celery and pancetta until lightly, but evenly, browned. Add garlic and chopped tomato, stir and cook for 2-3 more minutes.
Deglaze pot with madeira and white wine. Bring to boil, reduce heat. Simmer until reduced to almost dry. Add stocks, bouquet garni and return to boil. Reduce heat; simmer until reduced by half. Strain through a fine strainer into a smaller pot, bring to boil, then reduce heat, simmer until about 3/4 cup of liquid is left. Whisk in about 1-2 Tbsp softened butter, then finish with a little salt, cayenne pepper and lemon juice. Keep warm.

To assemble dish:
In a small medium sauté pan, heat butter and sauté mushrooms until lightly browned.
Stir in crayfish tails and herbs, and heat through. Pour in about 1/2 cup of finished sauce and stir. When hot, taste to adjust seasoning, then spoon over warm sweetbreads, sprinkle with chives and serve immediately.

Smoked Duck Hash

WITH RÉMY MARTIN COGNAC SAUCE.
PAIRED WITH RÉMY XO EXCELLENCE

METHOD

Melt butter in sate pan. When bubbling, add onion and celery dice and cook for 2 minutes, then add andouille and apple. Turn up heat and cook for 2 more minutes; add smoked duck and sweet potato. Sir and sprinkle with flour. Cook for 1 minute; add sherry and half of chicken broth, stirring to mix. Bring to boil. If mixture is too dry, add rest of broth. Add herbs and taste for seasoning. Mixture should be moist but not too wet. Cook for about 2 more minutes, remove from heat and cool.

To Prepare:

1 lb puff pastry, rolled out and cut into 12" squares
1 egg, beaten with 2 tbsp milk. Brush edges of chilled pastry square lightly with egg wash. Place 3 oz. (about 1/12) of filling in center of square and bring 2 opposite corners of square to meet in center. Bring other two corners to center to form small pyramid and pinch 4 seams to seal. Brush lightly with egg and refrigerate.

Cognac Sauce:

Combine first 4 ingredients in small pot. Bring to boil and reduce to 1 cup. Whisk in jelly and cognac and boil for about 2 minutes, or until mixture is slightly syrupy. Keep warm but not hot.

To Serve:

Pre-heat over to 450°f. Bake hashes packets for 12 minutes and serve with Cognac sauce.

INGREDIENTS

1 lb. Puff pastry, rolled out and cut into 12 4" squares
2 tbsp. butter
1/4 cup onion dices (1/4")
1/4 cup celery dice
1/4 cup andouille dice
1 cup green apple dice
1 cup smoked duck meat, diced
1/4 cup cooked sweet potato dice
3 tbsp. flour
2 tbsp. sherry
1 cup chicken broth
1 tsp. each chopped sage and thyme, preferably fresh
Salt and pepper

Cognac Sauce
2 ea. Shallots, minced
1 cup apple juice
1/4 cup apple cider vinegar
2 cups veal stock or stock made from smoked duck
2 tbsp. apple jelly
2 tbsp. Rémy Martin Cognac VSOP

BAYONA

Chef Greg Sonnier

GABRIELLE

About the Chef...

Greg Sonnier graduating with a degree in criminal justice, decided against taking up a beat on the streets, instead taking a beater in to the kitchen, by enrolling in a Culinary Arts Program. He was soon recognized by becoming an apprentice to celebrity chef Paul Prudhomme. After a successful stint at *Brigsten's,* Chef Greg and his wife, *Mary,* an accomplished pastry chef, opened their first restaurant, named Gabrielle, after their first daughter and his grandmother.

Since then the awards have rolled on including *New Orleans Magazine* –two of the "Fifty People to Watch in 1992;" the Great Chefs Series, "the New Garde;" *The Times Picayune,* "4 Bean" rating; *Orleans Magazine* – "The Best Chef in New Orleans" and "Chef of the Year," and in 1999 *Food & Wine* one of "the Top New Chefs in America." Greg has twice been honored with an invitation to cook at the prestigious James Beard House.

About the Restaurant...

Tucked away in the historic Bayou St. John neighborhood of New Orleans, sits a rare treat that's popular with well-heeled locals and strict gourmets alike. *Gabrielle*, a bistro-style restaurant that seats no more than sixty in the main dining room and enclosed patio, has clean and simple decor, but when you taste the food you'll understand why. There's nothing pretentious about this restaurant, no fancy window treatments or ornate ceiling fixtures to compensate for a nondescript menu, because the robust Creole and Acadian flavors coming from Gabrielle's kitchen, stand alone in making their bold statement.

Greg and Mary Sonnier, the most down to earth and accommodating couple you'll find in the business, met in 1984 while apprenticing under Paul Prudhomme at New Orleans famous kitchen, *K-Paul's.* Since opening in 1992, Gabrielle, named after the couple's daughter, has received rave reviews from the likes of Bon Appetit, Southern Living, Esquire, Food & Wine, and The New York Times, to name a few. But Greg wasn't always destined for the kitchen. He received degrees from Tulane and Loyola universities in criminal justice, before he began culinary arts training and luckily, for people hungry for quality Southern cooking, he has been doing justice to the palate ever since.

His Barbecue-Shrimp Pie as an appetizer is an incredible combination of big juicy shrimp piled high on a delicate short crust served with sweet potato mash. But a winner at our table was the Slow-Roasted Duck with exotic mushrooms roasted peppers and orange-sherry sauce over vermicelli rice noodles. The skin, cooked to a crispy perfection, creates a texture so complementary to the soft noodles. Braised Rabbit in port with dirty rice, crawfish and smoked tomato basil sauce is also a favorite, as is Pan-fried Trout with crawfish cornbread dressing and cheddar cheese Hollandaise.

And this family operation insists on dessert. Mary, as pastry chef, decorates light desserts such as the orange cake with edible flowers that grow just outside the front door, in the restaurant's herb and flower garden – truly a place where you can say "home sweet home."

Slow Roasted Duck

WITH ORANGE-SHERRY SAUCE. PAIRED WITH RÉMY EXTRA

METHOD

Preheat oven to 500°f. In large bowl toss onions with melted butter, season ducks inside and out with salt and pepper. Place 2 rosemary sprigs in each cavity. Tightly pack each cavity with onions and set ducks in a large roasting pan. Roast ducks for 10 minutes. Lower the temperature to 300°f and loosely cover pan with foil; roast ducks for about 4_ hours, draining fat every hour. Roast peppers directly over a gas flame until charred all over. Place peppers in paper bag for 10 minutes to steam, peel and remove seeds. Cut into strips. Blanch carrots for one minute then drain and put aside with peppers.

Discard fat from roasting pan; add orange juice, sherry, soy sauce and roast ducks, uncovered, for 30 minutes. Transfer to a platter and allow to cool slightly. Pour pan juices into saucepan, discarding any pieces of duck skin, skim fat off sauce and bring to boil over med-high heat. Reduce to 1_ cups; strain and return to saucepan. Halve ducks; discard onions, rosemary and all bones except leg bone, keeping breast attached to the leg. Re-warm in a low oven. Sauté oyster mushrooms in butter; add carrots, peppers and sauce; salt and pepper to taste.

To serve: Place sauce on plate with pasta or fried shoestring potatoes; duck on top, then garnish with vegetables and chives.

INGREDIENTS

2¼ lbs. Yellow Onions, Peeled And Coarsely Chopped
¼ lb. Unsalted Butter, Melted
2 Tbsp. Unsalted Butter, Solid
2 - 5 lb. Pound Ducks, Rinsed and Patted Dry
Salt and Freshly Ground Black Pepper
4 Large, Fresh Rosemary Sprigs
2 Medium Red Bell Peppers
2 Medium Carrots, julienned
2 Cups Fresh Orange Juice
1 Cup Dry Sherry
½ Cup Soy Sauce
4 oz. Small Oyster Mushrooms – Trimmed
4 Fresh Chives, Cut Into 1" Lengths
Serves 4

BBQ Shrimp Pie

PAIRED WITH RÉMY XO EXCELLENCE

METHOD

BBQ Shrimp Pie
   Process ingredients until blended. Taste for salt and sugar. Keep warm until ready to serve.

BBQ Shrimp:
   Brown small amount of butter in skillet: add pepper, rosemary and shrimp; add seasoning, and garlic; sauté over high heat until shrimp are pink. Add Worcestershire, beer and stock; bring to boil and allow liquid to reduce. Finish sauce by emulsifying butter into it.

To Serve:
   Fill tart shells with warm sweet potato mixture; arrange shrimp on top and then pour sauce over and around the pie. Garnish with a sprig of fresh rosemary.

INGREDIENTS

4 – 4½" tart shells
Sweet Potato Filling:
2 Lb. Sweet Potatoes (Roasted And Peeled)
2 Oranges (Zested and Juiced)
½ Cup Light Brown Sugar
Pinch Of Ground Cloves
1 Tsp. Vanilla Extract
1 Tsp. Cinnamon
Pinch Of Salt
Serves 4

BBQ Shrimp:
16 Jumbo Shrimp (Peeled In Center, Head And Tail Intact) About 2 lbs.
2 Tsp. Seafood Seasoning (We Use Chef Paul Prudhomme's Magic Seasoning)
1 Tsp. Finely Chopped Rosemary
1 Tbsp. Finely Chopped Garlic
1 Tsp. Cracked Black Pepper
4-6 Tbsp. Butter
¼ Cup Beer
1 Tbsp. Worcestershire Sauce
Juice Of Two Lemons
½ Cup Seafood Stock

GABRIELLE

Chef James Overbaugh

THE GRILL ROOM

About the Chef...

Chef *James Overbaugh* joined the Windsor Court Hotel from the famous California restaurant and winner of the coveted 'AAA' Five Diamond, Exxon/Mobil Five Stars, *Erna's*, in Elderberry House, located in the Relais & Chateaux Hotel du Sureau in Oakhurst, where he was both Executive Chef and General Manager.

Said Windsor Court Hotel General Manager Anthony P. McHale. "He comes from a property that has consistently offered one of the finest dining experiences anywhere in the world." The Elderberry under Jim's helm, was named by *Condé Nast Traveler* as the best in the country with a perfect score of 100.

Prior to the Chateau du Sureau, Chef Overbaugh was Executive Chef at the Stonehedge Inn at Tyngsboro, Massachusetts. He is a graduate of the Culinary Institute of America, New York.

About the Restaurant...

"Now what do I do with this?" (The late HRH Duke of Windsor – when faced with a bill after a long stay in a luxury hotel.)

The Windsors are a remarkable family. They have enjoyed Regal longevity and exude a certain anachronistic whimsy, which I for one have always associated with our royal family. And the charming **Grill Room**, at the Windsor Court Hotel nestled amongst the skyscrapers of downtown New Orleans, is certainly a regal place to dine. Taking great pride in the presentation of his food, Executive Chef James Overbaugh is the tour de force behind the critical acclaim that this stellar restaurant enjoys, including the Mobil 5 star AAA Five-diamond award, (the only one awarded in Louisiana, they proudly claim).

Overbaugh's diverse style that couples century-old methods and techniques with non-traditional ingredients, interprets well on the menus we are handed, with exceptional selections on the Chef's Tasting menu. Catfish Remoulade topped with Sevruga Caviar, or Sautéed Hudson Valley Foie Gras, sweet potatoes, perigord truffles and kumquats with rosemary were just two of the tastes offered along with the sommelier's pairing menu.

So far - so good. The ensuing entrees are generous and equally sating. My companion continues her "quest for the perfect Crab Cake", in this instance the Jumbo Lump Crab cakes with a saffron oil and herbsaint reduction. Her dreamy silence says it all!

All this, plus a majestic 10,000 bottle wine cellar which once released a bottle of Petrus '61 for $18,500.00 ensures that within this world class hotel there is this elegantly-disposed restaurant of quiet distinction.

Roasted Rack of Lamb

WITH LOUISIANA CHANTERELLE MUSHROOMS, SPINACH FLAN AND
MINTED FAVA BEAN RAGOOT. PAIRED WITH RÉMY XO EXCELLENCE

For the Minted Fava Bean Ragoot:
2 Tbsp. Unsalted Butter
1 Tbsp. Minced Shallot
1 Cup Shucked and Blanched
Fava Beans
1/4 Cup Rémy Martin XO
Excellence
1 Cup Reduced Veal Stock
2 Tbsp. Fine Diced Red Peppers,
Roasted, Peeled And Seeded
1 1/2 Tbsp. Chopped Mint
Salt and Freshly Ground White
Pepper

**For the Chanterelle
Mushrooms:**
2 Cups Louisiana Chanterelle
Mushrooms
2 Tbsp. Unsalted Butter
1/2 Tsp. Minced Garlic
1 Tbsp. Mince Shallots
Salt and Freshly Ground White
Pepper

**For the poppy seed potato
fingers:**
3 Medium Russet Potatoes
1/4 Cup Poppy Seeds
1/2 Cup Milk
1/4 Cup Semolina Flour
1/4 Cup All Purpose Flour
3 Egg Yolks
Salt, Freshly Ground White
Pepper and Nutmeg
1 Tbsp. Virgin Olive Oil

For the Spinach Flan:
2 Cups Fresh Stemmed Spinach
1 Cup Chicken Stock
1 Cup Thin Béchamel Sauce
1 Cup Heavy Cream
8 Eggs, Beaten
Nutmeg, Salt and Freshly
Ground White Pepper

**For the lamb and to present
the dish:**
4 Sides Rack of Lamb, 8 Bones
Each, Cleaned and Frenched
Salt and Freshly Ground
Black Pepper
1/2 Tbsp. Chopped Rosemary
1 Cup Japanese Bread Crumbs
1 Tbsp. Melted Butter
Salt and Freshly Ground White
Pepper
5 Tbsp. Dijon Mustard

METHOD

For the Minted Fava Bean Ragoot:
Melt butter in a medium sauté pan. Slowly sauté shallots. Add fava beans, season with salt and pepper, slowly sauté until done. Add Rémy Martin and simmer 1 minute. Add veal stock, reduce until sauce consistency attained. Add peppers and mint. Adjust seasoning.

For the Chanterelle Mushrooms:
Brush and remove any dirt or woodland particles from chanterelles. If mushrooms are large, tear into smaller pieces. Melt butter in a medium saucepan. Add garlic and shallots, sauté until translucent. Add mushrooms and sauté until lightly golden brown. Season with salt and pepper.

For the poppy seed potato fingers:
Preheat oven to 300°f. Bake potatoes until done. Remove, peel and cut into quarters. Press through sieve into large bowl. Grind poppy seeds in spice grinder. Transfer to small saucepot. Cook until completely dry. Remove from heat and transfer poppy seeds to bowl with potatoes. Add egg, cream of wheat and flour to potatoes. Mix together by hand until it becomes solid dough. Season with salt, pepper and nutmeg to taste. Bring large pot of salted water to boil. Dust hands with flour and pinch off 1/3 oz. pieces, roll them into 2" long fingers. Cook in boiling water for 3 minutes until done. Remove, shock in ice water and drain. Oil lightly to avoid sticking

For the Spinach Flan:
Preheat large pot of boiling salted water. Blanch spinach, shock in ice water, drain. Transfer to blender with sharp blade, add chicken stock and puree completely. Pass through fine strainer and transfer to a bowl. Whisk in béchamel, cream and well-beaten eggs. Season. Preheat oven to 250°f. Grease 8 two-ounce timbale molds with olive oil. Place timbales in small roasting pan, approximately 8"x8" and at least 3" in height, (the pan must be taller than the timbale molds). Fill timbales with spinach flan; mix until within 1/4" of top. Slowly pour very hot water into pan until water level reaches 1/2" from top of molds. Cover with tin foil and bake in over for 45 minutes.

Water surrounding flans inside pan should never exceed 185°f, as texture of flans may become bubbly and dry. After the first 30 minutes elapse, check flans every ten minutes by poking them with a small knife and it cleanliness. Once flans are done, remove from oven, uncover, and remove from water. Allow to cool, run a paring knife around flan to separate from mold and turn flans out onto a plate or pan for storage. Reserve.

For the lamb and to present the dish:
Preheat oven to 350°f. Season racks generously with salt and pepper. Preheat large cast iron skillet, add oil. Wait until faint haze is detected, place lamb in pan, eye side down, sear, turning frequently until done. Remove from skillet and transfer to roasting pan. Bake in oven until internal temperature has reached 100°f. Remove from oven. Combine rosemary, breadcrumbs, butter and season. Rub each rack with Dijon mustard and then coat evenly with breadcrumbs. Return to oven and cook for an additional five minutes until golden brown and lamb has reached an internal temperature of 125°f. Remove from oven and allow to rest 10 minutes.

Begin plating by arranging a warmed spinach flan, poppy seed potato fingers, fava bean ragoot and chanterelle mushrooms round front side of plate. Slice racks into four 2-bone pieces each and arrange two double chops per plate so they oppose each other as demonstrated in the picture. Place chops on plate and garnish with a mint sprig.

Pecan Cake

PAIRED WITH RÉMY XO EXCELLENCE

INGREDIENTS

For the Cake:
1 lb. 1 oz. Butter
1 lb. 10 oz. 750 Grams Sugar
13 Eggs
¼ Tsp. 8 Grams Salt
7 oz. Flour
½ oz. Baking Powder
1 oz. New Orleans Rum
1 lb 10 oz. Ground Pecans

Toffee sauce:
8½ oz. butter
13 oz. brown sugar
6 oz. corn syrup
1 tbsp. vanilla extract
1 tsp. salt
1 lb. 1 oz. cream

Chocolate tuille:
12 oz. butter
12 oz. brown sugar
12 oz. corn syrup
¼ tsp. salt
8½ oz. flour
8½ oz. cocoa powder
4 oz. cocoa nibs (optional)

Coffee ice cream:
1 lb. 1 oz. milk
1 lb. 1 oz. cream
6 oz. yolks
6 oz. sugar
7 oz. chicory coffee ground

METHOD

For the cake: Cream butter and sugar, add eggs one at a time. Add walnuts and salt. Add the sifted dry ingredients, and then the rum. Pour into greased molds and bake.

For the sauce: Combine all other ingredients except cream and boil for 5-10 minutes. Thin with cream and chill.

For the tuille: Melt butter, sugar, syrup and salt. Mix in flour, cocoa and nibs. Spread to desired size and bake at 300°f until crisp. Form out of the oven while warm.

For ice cream: Combine cream, milk and coffee in saucepan and bring to boil and strain. Whisk sugar and yolks to combine and temper into cream mixture. Cook to 185°f and strain over and ice bath. For best results chill for 24 hours before freezing.

To serve: Cover cake and sauce and heat in oven. Place small amount of sauce on the plate, cake on top. Scoop ice cream into tuille on the side of the cake and serve.

Chef Lidia Matticchio Bastianich

About the Chef...

Star of television series, *Lidia's Italian American Kitchen*, and *Lidia's Italian Table*, **Lidia Matticchio Bastianich** is the *"First Lady of Italian cuisine and restaurants in the USA."* Born in Pula, Istria, at the juncture of Italy and the former Yugoslavia, she arrived in New York in 1958. *Lidia's Italian American Kitchen,* began airing in January 2001 coinciding with her third cookbook (same name) just released in October 2001 (Knopf). *Lidia's Italian Table* was released in September 1998 together with its companion book (William Morrow, 1998). Among her many awards, are "Best Chef in New York" in 1999 by the James Beard Foundation, and the "Woman of the Year/Innovation Award, Restaurant category" from the Women's Institute of the Center for Food and Hotel Management.

In her free time, Lidia chaired UNIFEM Special Benefit for Recipes for Peace in 2001, co-chaired UNIFEM Special Benefit for the Women of Kosovo event in 1999, co-chaired UNIFEM Celebration of Women Charity event in 1998, and in 1994, founded Good Samaritan Hospital for the victims of the Bosnian war.

About the Restaurant...

"Celebrity chef" doesn't seem a grand enough title to encompass all that Chef Lidia Matticchio Bastianich has accomplished. She's the star of two widely popular television series "Lidia's Italian American Kitchen" and Lidia's Italian Table." She has several cookbooks under her belt, is the founder of an Italian tour company, has developed her own line of pasta sauces, and is a stellar restaurateur – her pride and joy being New York's **Felidia**.

When we arrived at the brownstone building it was Friday at 6 p.m. The mahogany open bar was peppered with young businessmen and women who'd fled the office to find refuge at this stylish yet refined establishment. Martinis in hand, guests packed the room with low laughter and chatter. Tables were filling up in both the downstairs and upstairs cozy Italian dining rooms, and appetizers were already being served.

Delicate choices on that particular evening were Pear and Fresh Pecorino Filled Ravioli sautéed with aged pecorino and crushed black pepper, or Istrian Wedding Pillows filled with Fontina, Asiago and Parmigiano-Reggiano cheeses, citrus rind and rum, savory reduction. Executive chef Fortunato Nicotra, the result of Lidia's careful searching in Italy, brings to the table tempting items, such as the succulent special Pan Roasted Black Sea Bass with celery, celery root, mushroom-tomato reduction, and poached morel.

Felidia also offers regional *Tasting Menus* which run for a month at a time and concentrate on the specialties of each Italian region – Tuscany, Piedmont, and others, pairing the wines of the region with the foods of the area. Such a menu leaves guests with not only a comprehensive experience, but also a thoughtful and expert education on a topic in which *Felidia Risorante* so clearly has a vast and extensive expertise.

Ravioli Stuffed With Pear

AND PECORINO CHEESE. PAIRED WITH RÉMY VSOP

INGREDIENTS

3 Bartlett Pears
3 Tbsp. of Mascarpone
1 lb. of Fresh Pecorino
2 Tbsp. Parmigiano
Reggiano
4 oz. Aged Pecorino
6 oz. Butter
Black Peppercorn

Fresh egg pasta:
3 Cups Unbleached All
Purpose Flour, Or
As Needed
4 Large Eggs
1 Tsp. Extra Virgin
Olive Oil
1/2 Tsp. Salt
Warm Water as Needed

METHOD

Grate pears and fresh pecorino cheese on larger part of grater. Mix with mascarpone and parmigiana. Prepare pasta (see below) pulling it very thin and into form of a rectangle. Place filling on one side and close ravioli. Melt butter with 8 oz. water. Cook ravioli in boiling water for 3 to 4 minutes. Finish with the aged grated pecorino and pepper corn flakes.

Fresh egg pasta:

Spoon 2²/₃ cups of flour into work bowl of a large capacity food processor fitted with metal blade. Beat eggs, olive oil and salt together in a small bowl until blended. With the motor running, pour egg mixture into feed tube. Process until ingredients form rough and slightly sticky dough. If mixture is too dry, drizzle very small amount of warm water into feed tube and continue processing. Scrape dough out of work bowl onto lightly floured wood or marble surface. Knead dough by gathering it into a compact ball, pushing the ball away from you with the heels of your hands. Repeat gathering and pushing motion several times, press into the dough, first with knuckles of one hand, then with other, several times. Alternate between kneading and "knuckling" dough until it is smooth, silky and elastic – it pulls back into shape when you stretch it. Process will take 5 to 10 minutes of constant kneading, slightly longer if you prepared the dough by hand. (Mixing the dough in a food processor gives the kneading process a little head start). Flour work surface and your hands lightly any time dough begins to stick while you are kneading.

Roll dough into smooth ball and place in small bowl. Cover with plastic wrap. Let dough rest at least one hour at room temperature or up to 1 day in refrigerator before rolling and shaping pasta. If dough has been refrigerated; let stand at room temperature for about an hour before rolling and shaping.

Divide dough into three equal pieces and cover with clean kitchen towel. Working with one piece at a time, roll pasta out on a lightly floured surface to rectangle approximately 10" x 20". Dust work surface lightly with flour; too much flour will make the dough difficult to roll. If dough springs back as you try to roll it, recover with kitchen towel and let rest for 10 to 15 minutes. Start rolling another piece of dough and come back to first one once it has had a chance to rest. Let pasta sheets rest, separated by kitchen towels, at least 15 minutes before cutting them. Roll each piece out to sheets about 30" long by 11" wide. Keep two of past sheets covered with kitchen towels and place third on work surface in front of you with one of long edges toward you. Arrange twenty of filling mounds in two rows of ten over top half of the dough, starting them about 1½" in from sides of dough rectangle, arranging them about 2½" from each other. Pat fillings into rough rectangles that measure about 2" x 1". Dip tip of your finger into cool water and moisten edges of top half of dough and in between mounds of filling. Fold bottom of the dough over mounds of filling, lining up dough to bottom firmly, squeezing out any air pockets as you work. With a pastry wheel or knife, cut between filling into rectangles approximately 2½" x 2". Pat lightly the tops of ravioli to even out filling. Pinch edges of ravioli to seal in filling. Repeat with remaining two pieces of dough.

Black Sea Bass

METHOD

For the celery root:

Peel celery root and boil sedeano rapa until it is hot. In a separate pan, put three tablespoons of oil and add garlic. Put celery root, flatten with a fork. Puree. Finish with Parmigiano Reggiano and parsley, salt. Clean celery and use only hearts. Boil, cut them and drown them in the reduction.

For the fish:

Cook fish from the part with the skin for three minutes. Turn over and cook on the other side. Put in oven and cook for another 3 minutes.

Assembly:

Using the deep plates: Put in broth then the puree of celery rapa and near the "drowned celery" accommodate the fish and vegetables then serve.

INGREDIENTS

Reduction:	**For the vegetables:**
3 Pounds Water	2 Heads of Celery Root
3 Tomatoes	2 Cloves Garlic
1 Stalk of Celery	1/2 Cup Chopped Italian
2 Onions	Parsley
Tablespoons Sugar	1 Spoon of Grated
Salt To Taste	Parmigiano Reggiano
Reduce until you have	Salt To Taste
two cups of liquid left.	3 Celery Stalks
	1 Tablespoon Extra Virgin
	Olive Oil

INGREDIENTS

2 lbs.13 oz. Butter	For the pistachio
2 lbs. Pistachio Paste	granache:
1 lb Egg Yolks	8 oz. Pistachio Paste
1 Cup Sugar	4 oz. Cream
4 Cups Whites	Using a food processor,
1¼ Cups Pistachio Flour	whip together until
6 oz. Flour	glossy.

Pistachio

MOLEN CAKE

METHOD

Melt together over low heat butter and pistachio paste. Whip together egg yolks and sugar until lemon colored. Whip egg whites until stiff. In separate large bowl, mix all ingredients together, folding gently until combined.

Assembly:

Grease 4 oz. tin cups and fill them up half way with batter. Scoop some granache in center. Fill with more batter. Bake at 375°f for about 15 minutes. Serve the dessert with chocolate sauce.

Chef Jean-Jacques Rachou

LA CÔTE BASQUE

About the Chef...

Born in Toulouse, France, **Jean-Jacques Rachou** has been working in kitchens since he was ten. He spent the first twenty years of his career honing his skills in the best hotel kitchens of France, Morocco, and Portugal. In 1963, turning thirty, he came to New York to take a position as sous chef at the world famous *Colony Restaurant*. He finally opened his own restaurant, *Le Lavandou*, in 1975.

In 1979, after making it a great success, Rachou seized the opportunity to purchase the venerable *La Côte Basque*. Fifteen years ago, Rachou made a stir in culinary circles for 'painting plates' using squeeze bottles for sauces.

Once known for his 'muscular' cuisine, Rachou says it's time to lighten up. The new menu features his classical French background and impeccable flavors, yet reflecting the modernization of the restaurant. Regarding La Côte Basque, Rachou says, *"it's a challenge: it keeps me young. I am 20 years old! It's rewarding to start over again."*

About the Restaurant...

Very much one of the original founding fathers of New York's world wide reputation for top echelon dining, Jean Jacques Rachou continues to outshine most of his contemporaries. His reputation as one of the most omniscient creators in the country has placed him and this outstanding French restaurant at the forefront of fine dining. But it was in 1980, having purchased the renowned **La Cote Basque** from America's father of French cooking – Henri Soule, that Rachou finally established himself with the New York dining scene, with brilliant replications of dishes that were quite simply of Escoffier class.

Rachou's magic show, never seem to diminish as the years roll by. If the mood is different he is onto it, if palates change, he is adept to it. His delicate interpretation of Classic mode of cuisine has entranced and captivated an international clique of patrons. The atmosphere is hushed in this mid-town dining room. The ubiquitous coastal scenes of the famous Bernard Lamotte murals along with the imaginative floral arrangements provide a vivacious contrepoint to the formal yet attentive mood. Indeed this is a restaurant of contrasts, a result of which is Rachou's inspired menu. Although there is an excellent value for money prix-fixe lunch, it is the a la carte offering that gets the taste buds going.

I doubt there is a better *terrine de foie gras* in the country and this together with the equally satisfying *Risotto aux Asperges et Fruits de Mer* – brimming with succulent shrimps earn their place as traditional signatures. And as for his treatment of Sôle Anglaise – heavenly! Pick of his signatures are the Filet Mignon Tournedos served with the finest seared *foie gras* with truffles, and a quite magnificent Roast Farm Chicken in a Tarragon Sauce. In a word – divine!

Desserts add a touch of frivolity to the dining experience, especially the delectable ices and sorbets (all made here) and a traditional staples such as the Chocolate Millefeuille and Praline Bavarian Mousse.

And then as a grand finale, there is the entrance of the man himself, as he slowly moves from table to table like a benign schoolmaster enjoying the fruits of his labour to a rapt class. This is ostensibly a serious food restaurant, but do we perceive a twinkle in this Master Chef's eye?

Jean-Jacques Rachou

Banana Tart

PAIRED WITH RÉMY 1738

INGREDIENTS

Yields:
4 Individual Tarts
8¹/₂ oz. Pastry Cream
³/₄ oz. Banana Compound
4 Tart Shells
4 Baby Bananas
4 Tuile Cookies
6 oz. Coconut Sauce
6 oz. Caramel Sauce

Sweet dough
9 oz. Unsalted Butter
4 oz. 10x Sugar
10 oz. All Purpose Flour
2 Large Whole Eggs
3" Pastry Ring ⁷/₈ Inch High

Coconut Sorbet
2 lb. 2 oz. Coconut Milk
1 lb. 1 oz. Simple Syrup

Pastry Cream
500 -Ml. Milk
1 Vanilla Bean
4 oz. Sugar
4 oz. Unsalted Butter at Room Temperature
2 Egg Yolks
2 Large Eggs
2 oz. Pastry Cream Powder

Coconut Sauce
10¹/₂ oz. Milk
7 oz. Heavy Cream
4 oz. Shredded Coconut
8¹/₂ Sugar
5 Egg Yolks

METHOD

Sweet dough: Beat the butter until very soft, mix in sugar, then the eggs. Add flour until combined. Chill dough, covered in refrigerator until firm. Roll out on floured surface until scant ¹/₄" thick. Cut out circles 4³/₄" wide. Place dough over ring. Lightly stick dough with fork. Cook on parchment sheet on cookie sheet on top of rack of preheated 325°f oven for about 10 minutes until brown. Let cook and remove rings.

Coconut Sorbet: Simple syrup: Combine 8¹/₂ oz. sugar with 8¹/₂ oz. water. Heat to 200°f. Mix syrup with coconut milk, chill in refrigerator and freeze in an ice cream maker.

Pastry Cream: Bring milk and vanilla bean to boil in heavy-bottomed pan. Remove bean. In a bowl combine sugar, yolks and eggs. Slowly stir ¹/₂ of hot milk into sugar and eggs, pour mixture into milk. Continue to cook on medium heat stirring with a whisk, without boiling until thick and coats spoon. Transfer hot mixture to mixing bowl. Mix in butter, on medium speed beat until cool and creamy, about 20 minutes. Chill in refrigerator.

Coconut Sauce: Bring milk and sugar to boil. Whisk sugar and yolks together until smooth

Filet Mignon Côte Basque

PAIRED WITH RÉMY XO EXCELLENCE

METHOD

Perigourdine Sauce:

Reduce 1 cup of Port wine with truffle juice, add some Demi-glace and one spoon of salted butter.

Turn carrots, zucchini, and yellow squash in a form of large olives. Cut some tips of asparagus. Blanche. Cut one slice of foie gras. Pan sear filet mignon in oven at 375°f for 6 minutes (for medium-rare). Sauté vegetables with a little butter. Put filet mignon in center of the plate; add foie gras on top and the mushroom head. Arrange vegetables all around plate and put the Perigourdine Sauce on top.

INGREDIENTS

1 Filet Mignon 6 oz	1 Sliced Foie Gras
1 Carrot	1 Tbsp Butter
1 Zucchini	1 Mushroom
1 Yellow Squash	
4 Asparagus	**Serves 1**

INGREDIENTS

Salade de Crabe et Homard	2 Tbsp. Crème fraîche
2 Plums and 2 Mangoes	2 Tbsp. Ketchup
3 Lobsters	1 Tsp. Worcester Sauce
2 Cans Jumbo Limb Crab	Chop Parsley, Tarragon,
1 Cup Mayonnaise	And Chives
	Serves 6

Salade de Crabe et Homard

PAIRED WITH RÉMY VSOP

METHOD

Mix last six ingredients together. When dressing is ready mix it with Crabmeat and lobster cut in dice. Put aside the lobster claw. Set up ingredients in a ring and place in the middle of plate. Peel and slice mangoes and plums and set them up all around the plates. Place lobster claw above the crab (see picture).

Chef Christian Delouvrier

L E S P I N A S S E

About the Chef...

Born near Toulouse, France, Chef **Christian Delouvrier's** first culinary influences were his mother and grandmother, who passed on family recipes and the pride in preparing good food. After graduating from the Hotel School of Toulouse, he went to work in some of the world's best kitchens, including *L'Archestrate* and *Café de la Paix*, in Paris.

Arriving in the United States in 1971, Chef Delouvrier spent the next seven years developing at New York City's finest restaurants. Later, Delouvrier opened the famed *Maurice* in the Parker Meridian, in collaboration with Chef Alain Senderens. It earned three stars from the New York Times in 1986 and was the first hotel restaurant to receive four stars from Forbes Magazine. In 1991, Chef Delouvrier opened *Les Célébrites* at the Essex House which instantly received a three star review from the New York Times. His recent triumphs at *Lespinasse*, place Delouvrier at the zenith of his profession.

About the Restaurant...

Most deserving of the high praise from the pundits, Christian Delouvrier reigns supreme at **Lespinasse**, located in the legendary St. Regis Hotel, in this most fashionable part of the city. His innovative *cuisine de terroir* is the result of many happy days in the kitchen of his mother and both grandmeres, where he fully understood the essential basic of traditional French cooking. Lespinasse deserves Delouvrier and vice versa. If ever there was a glove fit and a marriage so perfect, then, most assuredly, this must be it.

The Louis XV interior, a vivid reflection of the glorious days at the French court, is at once simply stunning – delicate gilt and hand-carved furniture and the sparkling white crisp knapery. Et voila! The menu reading like an encyclopedia for the indulgent, the signatures, so reminiscent of Brillat Savarin and later Auguste himself, mirror the understated passion for the perfect recipe.

Witness the superlative starter of Tuna Carpaccio, on green jumbo asparagus and ginger aioli served with a 1990 Pol Roger Brut rose. He also presents a version of a classic – Coquilles Saint Jacques with Thyme and Courgettes – indeed this Ravioli of Divers Sea Scallops with Thyme and Zucchini, was nothing short of sensational. At our tasting of this mini-banquet however, the highlight for my delighted and indeed,delightful, fellow pleasure-seeker and me, had to be the Braised Lamb Couscous – very much *a la Tunisie*. Pick of the desserts by Master patissier, Patrice Caillot were the Chocolate Plate of hot and cold chocolate varieties – especially a chocolate sponge with the hot chocolate sauce in the center – delish! The choice of the 1994 Chateau d'Yequem, was nothing short of "historic" (thanks Michael Winner! – Style Magazine restaurant reviewer and sometime film director).

Delouvrier has accomplished what some thought was the impossible, but then again there clearly is no substitute for effortless ability and in this man's case, absolute confidence.

Allez les Bleus! Bravo!

Lobster in Beurre Blanc

WITH LOBSTER RAVIOLI. PAIRED WITH RÉMY EXTRA

METHOD

Lobsters: Cook whole lobsters in boiling salted water for 2 minutes, shock in ice bath, breakdown claws, knuckles, tail, save bodies for other use. Cut tails in ½ Reserve claws and knuckles for Ravioli.

Vanilla Onions: Slice onions thin, add to pot 1½ tbsp butter, onions and vanilla pod and vanilla seeds; sweat over low heat until just cooked, keep warm until service.

Nage: Sweat shallots till translucent in clarified butter. Add squash sweat 4-5 minutes. Add white wine bring to boil. Add vin de paille. Boil, add Muscat, boil, add chicken bouillon. Simmer 45 Minutes, check for balance of flavors. Strain, chill, heat when needed.

Lobster Foie Gras Ravioli: Slice claws into ½" thick slices cut slices of foie gras approximately the same size. Place foie gras on wonton skin painted with eggwash, lobster on top of foie gras. Cover with another wonton skin press around to close. Cut with ring cutter. Heat in water when needed.

To Serve: Finish lobster in Beurre Blanc over very low heat. Heat Onions. Cook Ravioli. Place lobster on onions. Slice and fan one claw in separate bowl. Top with cooked ravioli, sliced scallions and about 3 tbsp of Nage. Add cooked Ravioli. Pour remaining sauce in with Ravioli.

INGREDIENTS

4½ Lbs. Lobsters
1 Quart of Beurre Blanc
2 Onions Sliced
½ Tbsp. Butter, Whole
1 Vanilla Pod Cut In ½, Seeds Removed
2 Butternut Squash Peeled, Seeded, Sliced
4 Shallots Peeled & Sliced
2 Tbsp. Butter, Clarified
1 Cup White Wine
1 Cup Vin De Paille
1 Cup Muscat Beaute De Venise
½ Cup Chix Bouillon
8 Wonton Skins
6 oz. Foie Gras Raw
1 Egg
4 Scallions Sliced On Bias

Cochon de Lait Confit

(CONFIT OF BABY PIG) PAIRED WITH RÉMY EXTRA

M E T H O D

Using rack or perforated pan, arrange half the pig in single layer. Cover with ½" of salt, 4 bay leaves and 11 cloves garlic. Layer remaining pieces on top and cover with ½" of salt, 4 bay leaves and 11 cloves garlic. Place rack over a pan to capture drippings. Meat should not come into contact with own juice. Marinate uncovered in refrigerator overnight. Discard drippings; lightly wash pork in water to remove all salt. Pat dry. There should be no moisture on meat. Heat oven to 325°f. Heat duck fat in large stockpot over medium heat to 180°f. Add pork and cover surface of the fat with circle of parchment paper. This seals fat and prevents any evaporation during cooking. Cook in oven for 3-4 hours or until meat starts to just pull away from bone. Check oven temperature from time to time to be sure it does not go above 350°f. Remove from oven. Raise temperature to 500°f. Remove pork from fat and drain on paper towels. Cut meat off bone into serving size pieces. Place pieces skin side up on baking sheet with sides. Cook until skin is crispy and golden brown.

Serve on serving dish. Veal jûs on the side. (pork jûs will offer too much of pork flavor). Serve dish of cassoulet on side.

INGREDIENTS

4 Each Lemons	4 Slices 2.5 oz. Each
4 Each Vanilla Beans	Foie Gras
¼ Of A Stick Cinnamon	*Salt To Taste*
2 Tbsp. White Wine	16 Each Dates
2 Tbsp. Honey	
4 Tbsp. Lemon Juice	**Reduction**
¾ Cup Water	1 Cup Lemon Juice
1 Cup Kosher Salt	1 Cup Honey

INGREDIENTS

1 Baby Pig, Quartered Into	8 Bay Leaves
2 Shoulders, 2 Racks,	22 Cloves Garlic, Peeled
2 Legs, 1 Double-Loin	1½ Gallons Duck Fat
2 lb. 3 oz. Coarse Salt	**Serves 12**

Foie Gras

PAIRED WITH RÉMY XO EXCELLENCE

M E T H O D

Blanch lemons for 3 minutes. To remove wax, marinate in salt for 2 days prior. Wash before blanching. Peel lemons, being careful not to take too much of the white part.

In saucepan, combine lemon peel, honey, white wine, vanilla beans, lemon juice, and cinnamon. Bring to boil, simmer until lemon is tender and liquid syrupy. Reserve.
In boiling water, blanch dates. Peel, process them in food processor. Reserve. In a sautoir, mix lemon juice and honey, reduce until syrupy. Let cool at room temperature. Sprinkle salt and pepper on foie gras. Reserve.

To Serve:
Warm up dates and lemon peel. Make circle with lemon and honey glaze on plate. Place foie gras on top of date puree.

Chef David Burke

PARK AVENUE CAFE

About the chef...

David Burke began washing dishes at a small New Jersey hotel. Enthralled with the business, he pursued an education at the Culinary Institute of America. Graduating with honors his first job was in Norway. He then worked in France at *La Rapier* in Mauvezin to support himself on a one-year eating tour of Michelin-starred restaurants. On returning to USA, Burke worked for Charlie Palmer.

After working a series of Michelin three-starred restaurants in France, Burke took over at the *River Café*, earning three stars from *The New York Times*. This caught the attention of Smith & Wollensky's Alan Stillman who asked him partner the opening of *Park Avenue Café*.

David's numerous awards include The International Food Festival Nippon Award of Excellence by the government of Japan, *Chef Magazine's* Chef of the Year, The Robert Mondavi Culinary Award of Excellence, the first ever Auggie Award presented by CIA, and the supreme award of the Meilleur Ouvriers de France.

About the Restaurant...

Some of you may recall, during the late 60's, notices and graffiti appeared around the streets of London announcing "Clapton is God" – such were the prodigious talents of guitar maestro Eric Clapton. It would not surprise me if the same proclamations were made about David Burke, who has demonstrated, yet again, the depth and quality of the home-produced graduates of the Culinary Institute of America.

The "Most Imitated Chef in New York" (Christian Science Monitor) and double winner of the Robert Mondavi Culinary Award for Excellence are just two of the reasons why *Park Avenue Café* enjoys its continual spotlight. Alan Stillman must revere the day that he appointed Burke as Executive Chef for this popular establishment.

With two cookbooks under his bejeweled belt, Burke brings to the table a consistency and ingenuity of style that offers simple recipes and yet complex flavors. And indeed, many of the items work very well, such as the signature Pastrami Salmon, a classic Rack of Lamb and the Foie Gras Lollipops with such vegetarian dishes as Mrs. Ascher's Steamed Vegetable Torte – further evidence of his well-versed range.

As for the ambiance, the Stillman whimsy is there for all to see, with patriotic Star Spangled Banner, authentic traditional American crafts, and huge urns of flowers and wheat. For the inquisitive who love to be entertained by culinary voyeurism, there is the spectacular glass-encased, "Chef's Table," with its theatre-kitchen and seating for ten-perfect for that degustation.

Avoiding the haute cuisine syndrome, Chef Burke has managed to combine his informative stints with some of France's Michelin-feted chefs and his American roots to present an uncluttered menu, where taste and presentation rank high on his list of priorities.

Smoked Salmon Lollipop

WILD MUSHROOM FLAN, PARFAIT OF SALMON AND TUNA TARTARS
WITH CRÈME FRAÎCHE. PAIRED WITH RÉMY VSOP (ICED)

INGREDIENTS

Smoked Salmon Lollipop
(For Smoked Salmon Mousse)
4 oz. of Cream Cheese, Room Temperature
3 oz. of Mascarpone Cheese
3-4 oz. Chopped, Smoked Salmon
Salt and Pepper To Taste
1 Tsp. Capers
1 Tsp. Red Onions

Wild Mushroom Flan
1/2 lb. Chanterelle Mushrooms
1-Pint Heavy Cream
4 Eggs
1 tbsp. Salt
Pepper To Taste
2 tbsp. Butter
1/4 lb. Smoked Salmon-Cut Into Slivers

Parfait of Salmon and Tuna Tartars with Crème Fraîche
1 Cup Crème Fraîche
2 Shallots, Peeled And Minced
4 Tbsp. Olive Oil
2 Tbsp. Chopped Capers
2 Tsp. Lemon Zest
4 Tsp. Soy Sauce
2 Tsp. Ground Horseradish
2 Tsp. Chopped Coriander
2 Tbsp. Chopped Chervil
10 oz. Ounces Yellowfin Tuna, Diced
10 oz. Salmon, Ground
2 Tsp Coarse or Kosher Salt
2 Tsp Freshly Ground Pepper
Olive Oil for Rings
10 oz. Osetra or Other Caviar (Optional)

Serves 10

METHOD

In food processor, pulse all ingredients until very smooth. Season to taste with salt and pepper. Using a pastry bag, pipe mousse into lollipop molds, insert sticks and chill. When set, remove from molds and wrap with very thin sliced smoked salmon. Can be sprinkled with herbs and poppy seeds, tiny toasted breadcrumbs.

Wild Mushroom Flan:

Simmer heavy cream with mushrooms for 6-8 minutes. Puree in food processor and strain. In a bowl, whisk 4 eggs, slowly adding cream and mushroom mixture while whisking. Season with salt and pepper. Reserve. Prepare 12-16 large eggs by removing top with egg scissors, emptying yolk and white (to be used for another use) and reserve shells. Rinse shells and remove any fragile pieces with your fingers. Fill each egg with approximately 3 Tbsp of mixture, or until 3/4 full. Place eggs back into egg carton and into baking pan with 1/2 inch of water. Cover pan with foil and bake in a pre-heated oven at 325°f for 45-55 minutes.
In a small sauté pan, melt butter, add corn and heat through. Add salmon and chives and warm gently. Add salt and pepper to taste and top each egg with small amount. Serve immediately in eggcups with espresso spoons.

Parfait of Salmon and Tuna Tartars with Crème Fraîche:

Whip crème fraîche until thick, and stiff peaks are formed. Reserve in refrigerator. Combine shallots and olive oil in small saucepan, sauté until shallots are translucent. Place shallots in a bowl and add capers, lemon zest, soy sauce, horseradish, coriander, and chervil. Mix until combined. Divide shallots mixture into two equal parts. Combine one half with diced tuna; combine other half with ground salmon. Add 1 tsp salt and 1 tsp pepper to tuna mixture and mix until all ingredients are combined. Add I tsp salt and 1 tsp pepper to salmon mixture and mix until all ingredients are combined. Lightly brush inside of 10 rings or molds with olive oil. Place waxed paper on a cookie sheet. Place molds on cookie sheet.

To Assemble:

Place 2 tbsp of tuna mixture in each mold. Smooth tuna mixture with back of spoon. Place 2 tbsp of salmon mixture on top of tuna mixture. Smooth salmon mixture with back of spoon.

Pastrami Salmon

PAIRED WITH RÉMY EXTRA

METHOD

Place salmon on a platter. Combine salt and sugar. Mix well, and coat both sides of salmon with salt mixture. Combine coriander, parsley and shallots in food processor and puree. Coat both sides of salmon with puree. Refrigerate salmon for 2-3 days. Scrape marinade from fish and discard. Dry fish with paper towels. Combine molasses, cayenne pepper and bay leaves in saucepan. Bring to boil and simmer for 1 minute. Allow molasses mixture to cool and using a brush, paint fish on both sides with mixture.

Sprinkle paprika, coriander, ground black pepper, and cracked pepper on both sides of fish. Refrigerate salmon overnight.

To serve: Cut Pastrami Salmon into thin slices on the bias, or diagonally, and serve with Mustard oil, rye toast, and if you wish potato pancakes.

INGREDIENTS

1 Side Salmon, About 2-2½ Lb, Skin and Bones Removed	4 Tbsp. Ground Coriander Seed
1 Cup of Coarse or Kosher Salt	4 Tbsp. Freshly Ground Pepper
½ Cup Sugar	4 Tbsp. Cracked Pepper
2 Bunches Fresh Coriander	Mustard Oil
1 Bunch Fresh Parsley	Rye Toast
½ Lb Pound Shallots, Peeled	Potato Pancakes (Optional)
½ Cup Molasses	
2 Tbsp Cayenne Pepper	Serves 10 as starter
5 Bay Leaves	Hors d'oeurves
4 Tbsp. Paprika	

INGREDIENTS

1½ Hardshell Maine Lobster	6 Pieces Potato Gnocchis
¼ Lb Sweet Butter	**Serves 1**
¼ Cup Sauterne Wine	**Gnocchis Ingredients**
1 Tsp Fresh Tarragon	
2 Pieces Asparagus *(Jumbo, Peeled And Blanched)*	2½ lb Potatoes - Baked and scooped out
5 Pieces Morels *(Braised In Rémy XO Excellence)*	4 oz. Cake flour
	4 oz. AP flour
1 Tsp. Shallots	½ cup parmesan cheese
1 Cup Lobster Stock	½ cup Chives
2 Lemons	1 egg
2 Tbsp. Extra Virgin Olive Oil	Mix together. Roll into a log shape. Cut into 1inch pieces and boil for 2-3 minutes. Drain water.
Salt and Pepper	

Butter Braised Lobster

PAIRED WITH RÉMY XO EXCELLENCE

METHOD

Blanch Lobster in boiling water and remove shell. In saucepan add butter, lobster stock, wine and reduce by half. Add lobster tail and 2 claws, reduce-until thick.

Place glazed lobster on top of asparagus, morels, potato gnocchis that will be sautéed.

Section 2 lemons-chop fine. Add salt and pepper to taste. Add olive oil and spoon on top of lobster.

Chef David Cunningham

PETROSSIAN

About the Chef...

As a teenager, **David Cunningham** dreamed of becoming a chef. With the help of his French brother-in-law, also a chef, David embarked on a learn-as-you-go journey through Paris. As David notes, "[his] food reflects what [he] learned in France. Europeans focus more on choosing, seasoning, and cooking than on presentation or melding."

During his first year in Paris, Cunningham got a job as a line cook at *L'Auberge de I'Ill,* a three star Michelin restaurant in Alsace. Initially he worked for free, until the family started to pay him. After a year, David moved back to Paris to work at the *Bristol Hotel.*

David found a position with Chef Gilbert La Coze at *Le Bernardin* upon returning to New York. Next, David accepted a position at *Lespinasse* with Chef Gray Kunz. He recognizes this time as the turning point in his career. *"Chef Kunz was definitely my biggest influence. He gave me the finishing touches I needed – especially the flair for presentation and the use of Asian spices,"* David says. Today his dishes and his uncanny knack of presentation and taste continues to place *Petrossian* at the pinnacle of East Coast dining.

About the Restaurant...

"The only thing to serve with good caviar is more caviar, and of course good champagne or iced vodka" – Armen Petrossian.

I originally reviewed this landmark restaurant in 1988. I enjoyed the city then, as did my son, on his school breaks. New York was his favorite city, **Petrossian**, his favorite restaurant, and brunch, his favorite meal. Hair slicked down like Alfalfa, "the little rascal" would be thoroughly spoiled by the then – Chef, Michel Attali, with his order of fluffy scrambled eggs, with a topping of sevruga, smoked salmon and toast points, served with as much ceremony, that a 10 year- old was entitled to! Indeed, when asked what my favorite meal is, I can unhesitatingly reply, *"Scrambled eggs, smoked salmon, caviar, toast points and a flute of champagne!"* as I wistfully recall those days, indulging my favorite person in the world.

Petrossian uncompromisingly maintains its dedication to refined decadence and excellence. These days, the talented David Cunningham is the chef. No stranger to a fastidious New York, with splendid stints at Le Bernadin, and Lespinasse, Cunningham has acquitted himself well and, with earlier apprenticeships at the great French chateaux with the Michelin icons, my, how it shows!

Naturally, there are the Petrossian hallmarks of Petrossian Teasers offering a selection, or La Tradition Petrossian, including a tasting of Smoked Salmon, Foie Gras and Sevruga, or the whole Lucullus experience "The Three Caviar Prince Gourmet Presentation" (15 grams each of; Sevruga, Ossetra and Beluga – a mere $120.00!) But it is Cunningham's versatility and savvy that are given the spotlight, with memorable menus that include a Crispy Skate Wing with spinach and arugula, brown butter and vegetable brunoise sauce, and sautéed Veal Tenderloin, sweetbread and tongue.

This divine extravaganza is complete with the trade-marked dessert, Blinchick Baicale, consisting of poached fig, caramel foam, fleur de sel, and Armagnac sabayon.

Seared Scallops and Duck Foie Gras

APPLE AND BACON SALAD. PAIRED WITH RÉMY VSOP

INGREDIENTS

12 pieces Deep Sea Scallops
12 1oz pieces
Duck Foie Gras

Salad
2 Granny Smith Apples
1oz Fresh Chives
1oz Crispy Bacon
1oz Hazelnuts
1/2 Oz Hazelnut Oil
Salt and Pepper To Taste

Sauce
1 Cup Apple Cider
1 Cup Cider Vinegar
1 Tablespoon Coffee
(Espresso)
1/4 Cup Hazelnut Oil
Salt and Pepper To Taste

Garnish
12 Pieces Apple Tuiles

METHOD

Salad:
Peel and dice apple, lightly sauté in butter and deglaze with Rémy Martin. Cool apples and mix with crumbled bacon, chopped chives, chopped hazelnuts, hazelnut oil, salt and pepper.

Sauce:
Mix cider and cider vinegar together in a saucepot and reduce by 2/3. Add espresso and using a hand mixer blend in the hazelnut oil until thick. Taste for salt and pepper.

Garnish:
Slice an apple paper thin into cross sections and dip into warm simple syrup with a dash of lemon juice. Lay on a lightly greased cookie sheet and let dry over night.

Scallops:
In very hot skillet sear foie gras. Once fat starts to render from foie gras add scallops and sauté until both are golden brown on both sides. Foie gras will be cooked first, place it on a paper towel to drain. Once scallops are cooked, remove them from skillet and slit them in the center 2/3 of the way through. Place foie gras into the opening.

To serve:
On a clean white plate, make three little piles of apple salad. Place stuffed scallops one on top of each pile and lay dry apple disc on top of each. Drizzle whole plate with sauce and serve.

Sautéed Veal Tenderloins

SWEETBREAD & TONGUE MORELS & ASPARAGUS
PAIRED WITH RÉMY EXTRA

METHOD

Sauce: Gently sweat chopped shallots in butter until transparent. Add morels and scraps, cook until tender. Deglaze with Madeira, reduce by half. Add heavy cream and half of veal stock. Simmer for 20 minutes. Strain and then reduce until slightly thick. Finish with salt and pepper and add the raw cognac at the end.

Garnish: Gently sauté morels until tender then add asparagus tips. Simmer until warm and season with salt and pepper.

Meat: Season pieces of tenderloins, sweetbread, and tongue and sauté gently in a sauté pan. When veal medallions are cooked remove from pan. With sweetbreads and veal tongue still in the pan, deglaze with Madeira and remaining veal stock. Let pieces simmer and baste them frequently as to glaze them.

To Serve: Shingle veal pieces on large white plate, starting with one piece of tenderloin then sweetbread, tenderloin, tongue. Then top meats with morel asparagus mixture. Drizzle sauce over and around the meat. Serve.

INGREDIENTS

8 2 oz. pieces Veal Tenderloin	1 Tbsp. Chopped Shallots
4 1 oz. pieces Sweetbread	1 Cup Heavy Cream
4 1 oz. pieces Veal Tongue	1/4 Cup Madeira
Sauce:	*Salt and Pepper To Taste*
1 Pint Veal Stock	**Garnish:**
2 oz. Rémy Martin	1 Pint Morels
1 Pint Morels and Scraps	1 Bunch Blanched Asparagus Tips

INGREDIENTS

5 Granny Smith Apples	**Puff Pastry:**
4 oz. Clarified Butter	4 scoops Caramel Ice Cream
3 oz. Brown Sugar	1 tbsp. Ground Pistachios
Pinch of Fleur de Sel	
1 tsp. Ground Cinnamon	

Apple Tart Fine

PAIRED WITH RÉMY 1738

METHOD

Lay four puff pastry discs on heavy sheet pan and prick with a fork. Peel and slice apples being sure to remove seeds and core. Lay them in spirals on top of puff pastry disc.

Coat them with butter, brown sugar, cinnamon and fleur de sel. Bake in a 375°f until golden brown. Remove from oven and serve very hot with a scoop of caramel ice cream and sprinkle with chopped pistachios.

Chef Brad Steelman

About the Chef...

Chef **Brad Steelman** studied hotel and restaurant management prior to attending the Culinary Institute of America in Hyde Park, New York. Upon graduating, he spent a year in Boston and then moved to New York City to be the sous chef at the acclaimed restaurant *Montrachet*. Approached by respected restaurateur Michael "Buzz" O'Keeffe, Steelman then joined the team at *The Water Club*. Some years later, he took over the kitchen at *The River Cafe*.

Other highlights for Mr. Steelman include cooking for Julia Child's 80th Birthday Celebration, The Grammy Awards, Chefs in America Awards and the fourth annual James Beard Awards. He also has appeared on numerous television shows, including demonstrations on the TV Food Network's *Talking Food* and In *Food Today*, and Lifetime TV's Our Home.

About the River Café...

No stranger to the critics' spotlight, Brad, **The River Cafe's** quite dashing maitre chef, adds the essential ingredient that sets a dramatic stage for this dining icon. Very much the David Bowie of the New York restaurant scene, River Cafe, particularly with Steelman's fingers on the pulse of food trends, has stayed so very much in tune with a fickle and impressionable industry.

The River Cafe, situated at the foot of the Brooklyn Bridge with the most breathtaking of views of Manhattan and its skyline, has to be the quintessential romantic venue. Indeed it is true to say that here is the perfect spot to start, develop or even finish a promising courtship! Whimsy and vivacity abound with unbridled ease on this raised barge, complete with portholes and huge picture windows.

We were privileged and delighted to let the Chef show us his recommended tasting menu. The Taylor Bay Scallops Ceviche, chilled in the half shell with sea beans, tomato and cilantro sprouts, and the Yellow-Fin Tuna, served with Asian pear and fire-cracker chilies, both set an impeccable tone that never once lost its way in an evening of surprises. These two items made for excellent choices, with the pairing of NV Drappin champagne from Rheims. But Steelman is also quite indulgent with his followers and clear illustration of this was his treatment of Handmade Potato Gnocchi with slow roasted pork shoulder, Parmigiana Reggiano Perigord, black truffle julienne in braising juice with carrot sauternes sauce and saffron pickled wild leek. Paired with a Riesling, the 99 Berncasteln, this was matchless.

And then temptingly, the piece de resistance, from a peerless patissiere- Ellen Sternau, made our visit all the more poignant, a taste-bud tantalizing array of desserts which included a chocolate replica of the Brooklyn Bridge. All so indulgent, decadent and unquestionably capturing the spirit of our memorable evening.

Most definitely, River Cafe *"you got us under your skin!"*

Pan Roasted Squab

GLAZED KOLRAHBI AND BABY CARROTS, CHESTNUT SPAETZEL, PINOT NOIR SAUCE. *PAIRED WITH RÉMY XO EXCELLENCE*

Legs and Sauce
1 Ripe Tomato, Chopped
1 Large Carrot
1 Stalk Celery, Washed
And Diced
1/2 Onion
1 Small Leek, Washed
And Diced
3 Cups Pinot Noir
2 Sprigs Fresh Thyme
1 Qt. Chicken Stock
2 Tsp. Canola Oil
Reserved Squab Bones

Chestnut Spaetzel
8 oz. Chestnuts, Roasted
And Peeled
4 Eggs
14 oz. All Purpose Flour
7 oz. Chestnut Flour
3 Cups Milk
2 Tsp. Chestnut Honey
1 Tsp. Nutmeg, Freshly
Grated
2 Tsp. Kosher Salt
1 Tsp. Fresh Ground Pepper

Vegetables
2 Small Knobs of Kohlrabi,
Peeled and Small Dice
10 Baby Carrots, Peeled
and Cut Oblique
1/4 Cup Chicken Stock
2 oz. Sweet Butter
Kosher Salt And Fresh
Cracked Black Pepper

METHOD

4 California squab: Breast removed with wing bones intact and skin removed from breast. Legs removed and Frenched, thighbone removed. Reserve bones for stock.

Legs and Sauce: In a large saucepot over medium heat place oil and bones, brown on all sides. Remove bones from pot and reserve. Add mirepoix and allow to slowly caramelize, add tomatoes and continue cooking for 10 minutes. Deglaze with 2 cups of wine and reduce by 1/2, return bones to pot, top with stock and thyme and simmer for 1 hour. In sauté pot over high heat place 1-tsp canola oil, season legs and brown on both sides, degrease pan and deglaze with remaining wine. Pass stock through fine sieve using back of a ladle to extract all liquid. Pour over legs and allow to simmer, frequently skimming the surface. Reduce stock until legs are cooked through and the sauce coats the back of a spoon. Hold warm.

Chestnut Spaetzel: In a saucepot bring milk and chestnuts to a boil, remove from heat and puree in a blender and allow to cool. Place remaining ingredients in a bowl. Make a well, using course wire whip mix in puree, mix until completely incorporated until mixture becomes elastic. Place mixture in refrigerator for 2 hours to rest. Over a large pot of boiling, salted water place spaetzel press 6" from surface of water. Poach spaetzel and refresh in salted ice water, dry and hold on a paper towel. Can be made 1 day in advance.

Vegetables: In sauté pan over medium heat place butter and allow to melt, add vegetables, season and allow to cook 3 minutes. Add stock and slowly simmer until stock has evaporated and vegetables are very tender. Adjust seasoning and hold warm.

Assembly: In sauté over high heat place 1 tsp of canola oil, season skinless breast and place in pan, allow to brown on both sides. Reduce heat and cook until interior is pink. Remove and allow to rest. In nonstick pan over medium heat place 2 tsp clarified butter, add spaetzel and allow to cook undisturbed until spaetzel begins to brown, flip and allow to continue browning. Adjust seasoning and fold in warm vegetables. In center of a warm dinner plate place spaetzel and vegetable mixture, top with breast and legs, nape sauce over breast and drizzle on plate. Top squab with braised chanterelle mushrooms (optional).

Crème Brûlée Banana Bread Pudding

METHOD

Crème Brûlée:

Bring heavy cream, 6-oz. sugar, vanilla beans and cinnamon sticks to a boil. Mix eggs, yolks and 6-oz. sugar together. Temper cream mixture into eggs and sugar. When all combined, strain through fine sieve

Banana Bread:

Mix oil, sugar and lemon rind. Add eggs, 1 at a time. Sift dry ingredients together. Alternately add dry and wet ingredients to oil mixture, adding bananas at the end. Bake at 350° until cake springs back and is golden brown. When cool, cube banana bread and rebake until toasted

Caramel Sauce:

Mix all sugar and corn syrup and add water until mixture reaches a wet sand consistency in a medium saucepot. Make sure no sugar is on sides on pot. Cook until mixture reaches a medium caramel color. Add heavy cream a little at a time using a wooden spoon to incorporate.

Assembly:

Line a hotel pan with aluminum foil (do not wrap foil around sides of pan). Using desired molds, place molds on top of aluminum foil and spray molds with Pam. Take about 3 cups cubed bread and mix with enough warmed Brûlée (can be warmed on stove or microwave) to make bread moist. Fill molds about ⅓ with bread and make sure to press into mold. Top with 3 slices of banana and a little caramel sauce (about 2 tbsp) and about 3 tbsp of Crème Brûlée. Fill hotel pan with water under aluminum foil. Cover molds and entire pan with aluminum foil and bake until set at 325°. When set remove aluminum foil and fill molds to top with Crème Brûlée mix. Let cool, unmold before service, dust top with Turbinado sugar and torch until burnt.

INGREDIENTS

Crème Brûlée

2 Qt. (8 Cups) Heavy Cream
6 oz. Sugar
5 Vanilla Beans, Split And Scraped
2 Cinnamon Sticks
6 Eggs (Whole)
6 Egg Yolks
6 oz. Sugar

Banana Bread

6 oz. vegetable oil
1½ Cup sugar
2 lemon rind
4 eggs
½ Cup milk
3½ cups flour
1 tsp. baking soda
1 tbsp. baking powder
1 tsp. salt
4 ripe bananas

Caramel Sauce

2 cups sugar
2 tbsp. light corn syrup
Water to consistency
1 cup heavy cream

Chef Erik Blauberg

About the Chef ...

Erik Blauberg's fascination with food began in his grandmother Clara's kitchen, leading to hands-on experience during his youth. After graduation, Erik learned quickly at the Imperial Hotel in Tokyo and Kicho in Osaka. This provided entrée into the kitchens of culinary legends Paul Bocuse, Alain Ducasse and Roger Vergé, where Erik perfected his own unique style.

Erik has worked in some of Manhattan's best-known restaurants, such as *Bouley*, *La Cote Basque*, *Windows on the World*, and *Tavern on the Green*. He briefly left New York to become Executive Chef of the Five-Star Jalousie Plantation Caribbean Resort in the British West Indies. Upon his return, he generated tremendous attention for his talents at *Colors*, and then as chef-owner of the critically acclaimed Soho-based *American Renaissance*.

Chef Blauberg has been recognized as "Culinary Master" by the Culinary Institute of America where he participated in the "Great Chefs Series."

About the restaurant...

I could live in *The 21*. I am unashamedly impressed with celebrity, and literati especially.

So, impressionable as I am, I was delighted to be seated in that iconoclastic of all dining establishments, "21". It was great to emulate "Papa" Hemingway by downing a hefty martini, surveying the masculine "clubiness" of the dark timbered panels and the racy red and white gingham tablecloths. Sinking into the warmth of the red leather banquettes, it was a cozy relief to take refuge in a club, where all diners are regarded as members, and appreciate Robert Benchley's immortal quip *"get me out of this wet coat and into a dry martini."* He must have encountered the same Arctic conditions of the blizzard, raging outside, as New York slithered to a halt, last winter, during our review.

Due to the inspirational master craftsmanship of the youthful Eric Blauberg, 21 has become one of the most celebrated dining venues in the USA and typically still attracts a clientele from the world of entertainment, the professions and the Street.

The classic menu includes such signature dishes as 21 Caesar salad with garlic croutons, Game Pot Pie, which is so flawlessly British, that it gives me fond memories of home. A Maine Lobster Salad with roasted potatoes, long beans and tomatoes had my companion in "seventh heaven", as did the stellar Pan Roasted Nantucket Seafood in a spicy shellfish broth, that undoubtedly warmed the cockles of her heart.

And of course, on hand, is a sommelier to keep the proceedings well lubricated. Choose from a Chateau Haut Brion or a classic Mondavi, or just a flute or two of Comte de Champagne from the dazzling wine cellar that recently won the Wine Spectator's "Award for Excellence," just as unequivocally, the restaurant has won ours.

Eric Blauberg

White Fallow Venison

WITH CHESTNUT PUREE AND LINGONBERRY TRUFFLE COMPOTE.
PAIRED WITH RÉMY EXTRA

METHOD

Rub venison with spice mix, season to taste with salt and pepper. Place venison into hot sauté pan with oil. Brown lightly. Add thyme sprigs, baste with spoon, add butter, continue to baste, cook for 4 to 5 minutes (for rare). Remove from pan, let sit for 1 minute before cutting into 3 pieces. Meanwhile, place chestnut puree in center of plate artfully. Place venison on top. Drizzle sauce around. Spoon celery root and carrots around. Artfully place Lingonberry Truffle compote around. Garnish with celery leaves and toasted pumpkin seeds.

Chestnut Puree:

In mixing bowl add potato, chestnut paste, butter, cream, season to taste with salt and pepper. Mix until smooth, careful not to oversize.

Chestnut Paste:

Place Chestnuts into 2 quarts salted boiling water. Cook until tender (approx. 10 minutes.) Remove from boiling water. Place on cooling rack until cook (approx. 20 minutes). Place into food mill and puree. Press through a tami with plastic bowl scraper. Reserve until ready for use.

Wild Lingonberry Truffle Compote:

In saucepan over medium heat, add lingonberries and vinegar, bring to boil. Season to taste with salt and pepper. Add Marjoram, stir in truffle oil. Serve with fresh truffles when ready to serve.

Chocolate Soufflé

PAIRED WITH RÉMY XO EXCELLENCE

METHOD

Melt chocolate and butter in a mixing bowl over heated double boiler. Stir constantly. Remove from heat. Allow to cool to room temperature. Slowly stir in the egg yolks until mixed well. In an electric mixer, add egg whites to a cold mixing bowl and whisk, slowly adding sugar until meringue is stiff – peak but not dry. Fold the stiff egg whites into the chocolate mixture until consistently mixed together. Cover with film wrap and refrigerate for 24 hours or until firm. Spray ramekins with vegetable oil, sprinkle them with granulated sugar, pour soufflé mix into molds until ½ filled. Place chocolate square in center, cover with soufflé mix until mold is ⅞ filled. Place soufflés into preheated 375°f oven for approximately 15 minutes or until soufflé rises and top seems firm. Remove from oven, dust top with vanilla sugar, serve with mixed berries, chocolate sauce and whipped cream or your favorite ice cream. Garnish with a sprig of mint.

INGREDIENTS

Serves 8
10 oz. Bittersweet
Dark Chocolate
5 oz. Sweet Butter
(Cut Into Small Cubes)
6½ oz. Egg Yolks
10 oz. Egg Whites
5 oz. Sugar
Vegetable Shortening, Pam
4 Tbsp Granulated Sugar
(For Sprinkling the Inside of the Molds)
8 Half Inch Squares of
Bittersweet Dark Chocolate
3 Tsp Vanilla Sugar
(See Pantry)
8 Tbsp Black Berries
(Cut Into Half)
8 Tbsp Raspberries
8 Tbsp Strawberries *(Sliced)*
1 Cup Chocolate Sauce
(See Pantry)
8 Tbsp Whipped Cream
8 Mint Sprig Tops

Chef Franco Barone

ANTONELLO

About the Chef...

Franco Barone has just the right recipe for success. As the executive chef of Antonello Ristorante, in Orange County, California, he blends the charm and tradition of the old world with contemporary Italian culinary concepts.

Originally from Sicily, Barone literally grew up in the restaurant business. He would spend hours in his uncle's restaurant. Under the tutelage of his gifted uncle, Barone developed into a discerning, creative and brilliant chef. When the cocky youth arrived in the United States in 1982, he assumed a position in the kitchen at *La Scala*, even though he had no formal training.

Barone's many honors include being recognized as one of the *Great Chefs of Orange County* by the Orange County Kidney Foundation and being nominated as *Chef of the Year* by the Southern California Restaurant Writers.

About the Restaurant...

Rated by **Zagat** as the "best Italian restaurant in Orange County," *Antonio Cagnolo's* establishment is like the proverbial candle, as it continues to draw a decidedly indulgent and chic Southern Californian crowd.

The purely theatrical setting and music from the "old country" add to the authentic Italian atmosphere. *Antonello* is a classic combination of both fun and romance, and it is here that you feel the timelessness and warmth of Northern Italy. If it is tranquillity that you seek, then opt for one of the many private dining rooms, which range from the rustic to the stately in theme.

Antonio's passion is evident in the food he offers and also in his love for art. Indeed, many works of his good customer and friend, *Aldo Luongo*, lend spectacular whimsy to the proceedings.

But do not forget the inspirational menu, which is a true celebration of Antonio's origins *"the escarpments of Italy."* From the dazzling array of appetizers, including a signature Bresaola con Soncino e Arugula, that literally *"melts in your mouth"*, and an exemplary Zuppa di Pesce – assorted seafood in white wine broth, to a full range of pasta, risotto and filet mignon. Whatever your fancy, it is highly unlikely that you will be disappointed with the food from the inspired cooking of executive-chef *Franco Barone*.

As for the grand finale – watch out for an almost choreographed performance, as an indulgent and enthusiastic wait-staff conducts, table-side, a preparation of such classics as flambe Crepes Suzettes and the best Zabaglione this side of Tuscany!

And speaking of performances, for you avid South Coast Performing Arts attendees, you can comfortably enjoy a reasonably priced pre-theatre menu, before being whisked away by the complimentary shuttle, in time for "curtain up" at the nearby center.

Lombata Di Vitellina Al Marsala

METHOD

Combine flour, salt, pepper in mixing bowl. Dredge veal chop in flour mixture. Set aside. In large pan heat butter to medium high temperature. Brown veal and sear until golden on both sides. Remove from pan. Drain out all but 2 Tbsp. of butter. Turn heat to high. Once pan is very hot. Sauté shallots until very lightly brown. Add porcini mushrooms, continue to sauté stirring until all mushrooms are evenly browned. Deglaze with Marsala and reduce slightly. Add seared veal and beef stock. Place in preheated oven at 350°f for approximately 20-25 minutes. Remove from oven, season with salt and pepper to taste.
Serve as desired.

INGREDIENTS

1 Cup Flour
1 Tsp. Salt
1 Tsp. Ground Black Pepper
6 10-12 oz. (each) Veal Chop (Bone In)
3 Cups Clarified Butter

1 Tbsp. Shallots (Finely Chopped)
1/2 lb. Porcini Mushrooms
(Cleaned And Sliced)
1-1½ Cup Marsala Wine *(Sweet & Dry)*
2 Cups Beef Stock
Salt and Pepper To Taste
Serves 6

Pan Seared Sea Scallop

AND SMOKED SALMON SALAD.
PAIRED WITH RÉMY EXTRA

Insalata Mista Cape Santle Salmone Affumicato

Pre-heat sauté pan with olive oil. Add minced shallots and slightly brown. Add scallops and brown on both sides. Finish with chopped parsley, add salt and pepper to taste. Arrange Smoked Salmon and Scallops on large salad plate. Toss mixed baby greens in lemon and olive oil. Place in center of plate. Garnish with shaved Parmesan cheese and toasted pinenuts.

INGREDIENTS

Serves 4

8 Sea Scallops Cut Into Halves	1/2 Cup Extra Virgin Olive Oil
12 oz. Baby Mixed Greens	Salt / Pepper To Taste
1 Tbsp. Minced Shallots	1/2 Cup Shaved Parmesan Cheese
3 Tbsp. Chopped Parsley	1/2 Cup Toasted Pinenuts
4 Tbsp. Lemon Juice	12 oz. Smoked Salmon

INGREDIENTS

Serves 4-6

1/4 Cup Brandy	5 Egg Yolks
1 Vanilla Bean	3/4 Cup Sugar
3 Cups Heavy Cream and 1 Cup Milk	15 Slices Bread, 3/8 Inch Thick, Crusts Removed Or Quartered

Buddino Di Pane

PAIRED WITH RÉMY VSOP

Split vanilla bean in half lengthwise with a pairing knife. Scrape seeds from pod. Combine them with the pod, cream, milk and brandy in a heavy saucepan. Scald the cream and milk, remove from heat, and set aside uncovered. Preheat the oven to 300°f. Strain cream and discard pod. Whisk eggs with sugar in a mixing bowl. Very slowly, add hot cream to yolks, whisking constantly. Arrange bread in 6-8 oz. Soufflé dishes. Pour custard mixture over bread, submerging slices with a spoon so they soak up some of the liquid. Place soufflé dishes in a baking pan, and fill pan with enough hot water to come halfway up the side of soufflé dish. Bake pudding in its water bath for 25 to 35 minutes, until edges have set and the center is still a bit runny. The pudding will continue to cook out of the oven and will set completely as it cools. Serve the bread pudding warm.

Chef Laurent Méchin

P A V I L I O N

About the Chef...

French-born chef, Chef, *Laurent Méchin*, who was valedictorian at the Gevigney Culinary School near Paris where he was trained, served an apprenticeship at *L'auberge de Chavannes*, a Michelin started establishment. His energy and enthusiasm is still apparent, despite the fact he is a 20-year veteran of the industry. The trilingual Chef made his way through some of the best restaurants and hotels in France, England and Switzerland then headed west to California where his experience includes the well-known *Pascal* restaurant in Newport Beach and *La Cachette* in Beverly Hills.

Consistently ranked by the *Zagat Survey* as one of the top ten restaurants in Orange County for food, décor and service, Pavilion continues as a local favorite for the past 15 years. With spectacular ease, Chef Laurent has adjusted the menu to reflect his style without compromising signature dishes.

About the Restaurant...

And the greatest show in Southern California, *Pavilion* at the Four Seasons Hotel, in Newport Beach, enjoys its extended run, under master chef Laurent Méchin. The continuing accolades are myriad : Wine Spectator award for Excellence,1999, Di RoNA (ninth consecutive year!) Zagat (number 1 in Orange County 2002). Laurent Méchin has vision and talent and with unerring and consistently ease, hits the mark with an inspired and delightfully eclectic cuisine- so much in keeping with the discerning palates of a well-heeled group of the area's "movers and shakers".

Dining here is one of life's great pleasures, enhanced by surroundings in a veritable oasis of such tranquillity, that the bustle and hustle of neighboring Fashion Island, a landmark mall, seems light years away. Lush floral exotica, artwork and an airy dining room are the constituents of a most memorable experience.

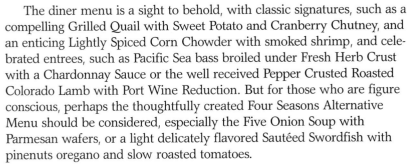

The diner menu is a sight to behold, with classic signatures, such as a compelling Grilled Quail with Sweet Potato and Cranberry Chutney, and an enticing Lightly Spiced Corn Chowder with smoked shrimp, and celebrated entrees, such as Pacific Sea bass broiled under Fresh Herb Crust with a Chardonnay Sauce or the well received Pepper Crusted Roasted Colorado Lamb with Port Wine Reduction. But for those who are figure conscious, perhaps the thoughtfully created Four Seasons Alternative Menu should be considered, especially the Five Onion Soup with Parmesan wafers, or a light delicately flavored Sautéed Swordfish with pinenuts oregano and slow roasted tomatoes.

Desserts add a touch of fun and frolic to the formal surroundings with Pear Gratin in phyllo pastry, and a to-die-for chocolate Banana Macaroon Mouse Cake and the irreplaceable Pinenut Ice cream with a sinfully rich chocolate sauce.

Méchin a native of Gascon in France, has earned his 5 star right to rule at this restaurant with creative displays and a panache, so reminiscent of many of the Michelin – starred super chefs from the distinguished chateaux of France. *Prenez garde* Roubechon, Ducasse et al, there is much of France right here in our own backyard.

Lobster Tartlet with Porcini Mushrooms

AND CHIANTI LOBSTER SAUCE RÉMY EXTRA.
PAIRED WITH RÉMY 1738

INGREDIENTS

Serves 4
For the Lobster
2 Maine lobsters
Steam lobsters and pull separated tails and claws. Remove shells form tails and cut into 1/4 inch slices. Break claws and knuckles with a mallet and remove the shell with a pair of scissors.

For the Lobster Sauce:
Heads And Shells From The 2 Lobsters, Cut Into Quarters
2 Tbsp. Tomato Paste
1 Diced Carrot,
1 Celery Stack, Diced
1/2 Onion, Diced
1 Leek Chopped *(Green Part Left From Julienne)*
1 Head Garlic, Smashed
2 oz. Rémy Martin Cognac
1 Bottle Good Chianti
1 Bouquet *(1 Bay Leaf, Thyme And 1 Bunch Parsley Stems Tied With Butcher Twine)*
32 oz. Fish Stock Or Clam Juice
4 Tbsp. Butter

For the Tartlet
4 x 4 Inch Baked Puff Pastry Disks
4 Ea. Porcini Mushrooms
1 Leek *(White Part Only)* Washed And Julienned
1 Tbsp. Minced Shallots
1 Tsp. Chopped Garlic
3 Roma Tomatoes Peeled, Seeded And Diced
1 Tbsp. Chopped Parsley And Chives

METHOD

For the Lobster Sauce:
Sauté lobster bodies in hot olive oil till lightly browned, add vegetables and sweat for 5 minutes, add tomato paste and cook 3 more minutes. Flambé with cognac and deglaze with Chianti, reduce and add stock and bouquet. Reduce to approx 2 cups, strain with a fine Chinois, return to heat and whisk the butter in.

For the Tartlet:
Slice and sauté mushrooms in hot olive oil, lower heat and add leek, garlic, shallots and cook until vegetables are soft. Season with salt and pepper, fold diced tomatoes and shopped herbs and keep warm. Place puff pastry in middle of plate. Scoop some mushroom mix on top of pastry and arrange lobster medallions around, garnish with a lobster claw, antenna and basil leaf.

Roasted Colorado Lamb Loin

METHOD

For the Lamb:
Remove bones form the rack and reserve them for sauce. Remove excess fat and sinew from meat. Season lamb loins and sear on all sides in very hot sauté pan with olive oil. Allow meat to cool on a rack. Brush with mustard and roll through pepper-breadcrumb mix,

For the Sauce:
In a very hot pan, brown lamb bones ¾ of the way. Add mirepoix and caramelize. Drain the rendered grease fat and deglaze pan with 2 cups of Port wine. Reduce to sec and add demi glace and aromatic herbs. Cook on medium heat till sauce is thick enough to cover the back of a spoon. Add remaining Port, strain and return to heat. Whisk in butter and adjust seasoning to taste.

Bake the lamb in 375°f oven to desired doneness; serve with garlic, chives mashed potatoes.

INGREDIENTS

Serves 4

For the Pepper Crust:
1 Cup Bread Crumbs
¼ Cup Chopped Herbs
(Rosemary, Thyme and Parsley)
½ Cup Crushed Peppercorns
(Pink, Green, Black And White)
1 Tsp. Salt
Combine all well

For the Lamb:
2 Racks of Colorado Lamb
1 tsp. Dijon Mustard
Salt

For the Sauce:
Bones From the 2 Lamb Racks,
Cut Into Small Pieces
3 Shallots, Minced
½ Diced Carrot,
1 Celery Stack, Diced
½ Onion, Diced
1 Cup Mushroom (Sliced)
1 Bay Leaf,
1 Tsp. Black Peppercorn
3 Ea. Thyme and Parsley Sprigs
3 Cups Port Wine
3 Cups Veal Demi Glace
2 Tbsp. Butter

Chef Richard Reddington

AUBERGE DU SOLEIL

About the Chef...

An educational backpacking European trip has become an accomplished culinary career, spanning high-profile restaurants in San Francisco, Paris New York – and now, Napa Valley. At 36, *Richard Reddington,* has become one of the nation's brightest young chefs.

Reddington is energy personified. He cultivated his talents at influential kitchens here and abroad. He previously cooked in San Francisco at *La Folie, Postrio,* and *Rubicon*; and then at *Arpége* in Paris, *Roger Vergé* in Provence, and *Pierre Orsi* in Lyon; came to New York to work at *Restaurant Daniel* and *Park Avenue Café* and returned to California to be sous - chef at *Spago*, in Beverly Hills.

An indication of Reddington's determination is demonstrated very early on, when he sent letters to twenty chefs, asking to apprentice without pay. *Roland Passo*t of La Folie offered him just one day. Two months later, Reddington was on the payroll, and he's been cooking ever since!

About the Restaurant...

"A good eater must be a good man, for a good eater must have a good digestion and a good digestion depends upon a good conscience" – **Benjamin Disraeli**, British statesman

In all good conscience, one cannot leave the wine country without a visit to this landmark *Le Relais & Chateau*. England has its *Le Manoir aux Quat' Saison*s and America must surely be thankful for having this establishment as its equivalent. This year is the season of comebacks for Northern California's older stars. In San Francisco, already *Masa's* is making the critics sit up and take notice once again. The same is true of **Auberge du Soleil**.

An inspired appointment of the talented Richard Reddington, himself no stranger to the kitchens of *Postrio*, David Burke's *Park Avenue Café* and Daniel Boulud, has led to a spectacular renaissance in the continuing history of this unique property. Romantically secluded at the top of a winding folly, with the sun-dappled backdrop of the surrounding Napa vineyards, it is no wonder that this restaurant and inn has become a favorite venue for not only star-crossed lovers but also the discriminating Epicurean.

Pick of his starters are the Caramelized Diver Scallops with cauliflower, almonds and capers or a very satisfying Sautéed Foie Gras with warm brioche and candied pistachios. Drawing on his blend of French, Mediterranean and Contemporary influences, Chef Reddington must be applauded for some of his more ambitious attempts including a Roasted Squab with a Brioche Stuffing and confit giblet jus, and the succulent Napa Valley Baby Lamb with tarragon gnocci and spring vegatables.

One thing is assured; it will be a long, long time before the pundits and critics ever consider writing off this exemplary wine country restaurant again! *Vive l' Auberge du Soleil!* May your sun continue to shine!

Chocolate Cognac Cake

PAIRED WITH RÉMY 1738

INGREDIENTS

Chocolate Sponge Cake
1 Cup Milk
2 Cups Eggs
$^1/_2$ Cup High Ration Shortening
1 Tsp. Vanilla Extract
Whip for 2 minutes

Sift together:
14 oz. Cake Flour
$^1/_3$ Cup Cocoa Powder
$^1/_2$ oz. Baking Powder
1 Tsp. Baking Soda
12 oz. Sugar

Add to liquid mixture and whip for 10 minutes. Bake at 350°f for approximately 45 minutes.

White Chocolate Mousse:
$^3/_4$ Sheet of Gelatin (Bloomed)
$^1/_2$ Cup Cream; Bring to Boil with Bloomed Gelatin
2 Cups Cream, Whipped To Soft Peaks
12 oz. White Chocolate
1 oz. Rémy Martin Cognac

Pour boiling cream over Chocolate. Add Cognac and stir until all chocolate is melted. Fold in cream. Set aside.

Ganache:
2 Cups Cream
16 oz. Chocolate

Bring Cream to a boil. Pour over chocolate. Stir to melt. Strain and set aside.

Milk Chocolate Mousse:
$^1/_2$ Cup of the White Chocolate Mousse
$^1/_4$ Cup of the Warm Ganache
Fold in together

METHOD

To Assemble:
In a $2^1/_2$" x $1^3/_4$" metal ring, place a $^1/_2$" thick disk of Chocolate Sponge Cake. It should fit snug inside the ring mold. Sprinkle with Rémy Martin Cognac. Add 2 tbsp of warm Ganache. Top with another sponge cake circle. Add 2 tbsp White Chocolate Mousse. Add another sponge circle and add 2 tbsp Milk Chocolate Mousse. Fill to the top of the ring and freeze for 2 hours. Unmold by heating up the ring slightly and push the cake through. Top with warm Ganache and serve chilled with Crème Anglaise.

Duck Breast

WITH BRAISED ENDIVES, TANGERINES AND A COGNAC /
GREEN PEPPERCORN SAUCE. PAIRED WITH RÉMY VSOP

METHOD

Add maple syrup to pan and caramelize slightly. Deglaze
with tangerine and lemon juices. Reduce by half. Add
Cognac and reduce by half. Add veal stock; simmer for 30
minutes until sauce thickens. Add peppercorns and finish
with butter. Season duck breast with salt and pepper.
Julienne endive and cook slowly in butter with ½ tsp sugar,
salt and pepper for 10 minutes until soft and cooked
through. Heat skillet; put in duck breast, skin side down.
Cook on skin side for 7-8 minutes until skin is rendered.
Turn duck over for 1-2 minutes for medium rare. Let duck
rest. Slice and serve over endive. Add tangerine segments to
sauce and warm gently. Spoon mixture over duck and garnish with chives.

INGREDIENTS

4 Boneless Duck Breasts, Skin On, About 6 oz. Each	¼ Cup Tangerine Juice
Salt and Pepper	¼ Cup Lemon Juice
6 Tangerines, Peeled and Cut into Segments. Reserve Juice for Sauce	1 Cup Veal Stock
	3 Tbsp. Butter
	2 Tbsp. Green Peppercorns
6 Heads Belgium Endive	1 Cup Rémy Martin
4 Tbsp. Maple Syrup	1 Bunch Chives

INGREDIENTS

1 lb. Foie Gras, Cleaned And Deveined
3 lbs. Rock Salt
1 Cup Toasted Pistachios
12 Cup Port, Reduced To Syrup
1 Tsp. Salt
½ Tsp. White Pepper
Pinch Of Sugar
¼ Cup Rémy Martin
Cheesecloth
Toasted Baguette Slices

Torchon of Foie Gras

WITH PISTACHIOS AND PORT SYRUP.
PAIRED WITH RÉMY VSOP

METHOD

Season Foie Gras with salt, pepper, and sugar, pour Rémy
Martin over it. Cover in plastic wrap. Refrigerate overnight.
Roast pistachios for 8 minutes in 350°f oven until slightly
toasted. Crush coarsely with back of a knife. Lay cheesecloth
on workspace. Lay Foie Gras on top and begin to roll to create tight cylinder 2 inches in diameter. Turn both sides of
cheesecloth simultaneously to create a compact roll. Put half-
salt in container, cover with remaining salt and refrigerate for
20 hours. Remove from salt. Lay out plastic wrap. Spread out
pistachios. Roll Foie Gras to coat. Roll back up in plastic.

To serve: Cut slices of Foie Gras. Serve with salad and
toasted bread. Garnish with pistachios and port syrup.

Chef Michael Patton

BRIX

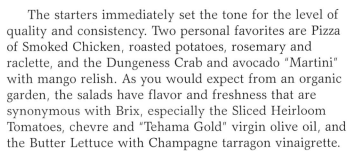

About the Chef...

A graduate of the Culinary Institute of America, New York, **Michael Patton** honed his skills in some of the country's most prestigious dining establishments. He perfected his style at the *Mansion on Turtle Creek*, *the French Room* at Hotel Adolphus, in Dallas, Texas, and the *1789* in Washington D.C. He was previously at *Four Seasons Hotel* in Beverly Hills, and the *Bellagio Hotel* in Las Vegas.

Patton is a participant in several local charities and has appeared at the James Beard House and on the TV Food Network with Robin Leach.

"I am delighted to bring my philosophy to Brix. Food is a shared human experience, one element that we all have in common. To me, as a chef I try to foster this image. Good food should bring out good conversation and kinship. Brix is going to epitomize everything that I have learned during my career."

About the Restaurant...

Great things will soon be written about the new "young Turk", Chef Michael Patton, at this exceptional wine restaurant. The appeal of dining at **Brix**, whether al fresco, or in the main dining room, is as much the ambiance and décor, as the food and service. Soaring, oak-beamed ceilings and flagstones help create the desired rustic feel. Yet, subtle hints of Italianate accents and soft interior décor create a look of simple modernism. The result is a well-conceived and balanced interior.

The theatre kitchen contains the prodigious talents of Chef Patton. Providing a clear illustration of why the restaurants of Napa have such tremendous esteem, the menu is a spotlight on American modern cooking, and certainly, the chef's pedigree!

The starters immediately set the tone for the level of quality and consistency. Two personal favorites are Pizza of Smoked Chicken, roasted potatoes, rosemary and raclette, and the Dungeness Crab and avocado "Martini" with mango relish. As you would expect from an organic garden, the salads have flavor and freshness that are synonymous with Brix, especially the Sliced Heirloom Tomatoes, chevre and "Tehama Gold" virgin olive oil, and the Butter Lettuce with Champagne tarragon vinaigrette.

Their entrees offer something for individual tastes and preferences. Of particular gratification was the Grilled Prime New York Strip Steak and ox-tail red wine sauce, and the Roasted Mahi Mahi on fingerling potato, oyster mushroom with caviar leek cream. If you have a busy winery itinerary, for lunch, opt for a great sandwich, especially the Rotisserie Leg of Lamb, organic watercress, Bermuda onion and goat-cheese Tzatziki.

Further evidence of their enterprise is the en-suite gift shop, which offers a gorgeous array of gifts, linens, candles and fine wines. Oh, and "happy day" – no cell phones! (truly leaving one *"far from the madding crowd"*).

Ox Tail & Forest Mushroom Fricassee

WITH SPRING LEEKS AND TRUFFLE POLENTA. PAIRED WITH RÉMY XO EXCELLENCE

METHOD

Season ox tail with salt and pepper, dust with flour and sear in olive oil, until all sides are brown. In a heavy bottom saucepot sauté onions, carrots, celery with olive oil until caramelized. Add chopped thyme and garlic cloves. Deglaze pot with cabernet and Rémy Martin XO Ecellence. Reduce by half. Place seared ox tail in pot and cover with veal stock.

Braise ox tail in a 350°f oven until meat is tender and falling off the bone. Remove ox tails from pot and reduce sauce. Clean meat from bones and reserve. Sauté mushrooms with minced shallots in separate pans. Do not mix until they are cooked. Blanch spring leeks and reserve. In a saucepot add ox tail, mushroom and reduced sauce. Simmer this mixture 30 minutes (to incorporate flavors.) Gently add spring leeks. Add chopped parsley and adjust seasoning. In a warm bowl place the disk of seared truffle polenta.

Place a generous portion of the ox tail fricassee on top of the polenta. Garnish with fried parsnips.

INGREDIENTS

Serves 6
6 Ox Tail
(Trimmed of Excess Fat)
2 Ea. Spanish Onions
2 Ea. Carrots
2 Ea. Celery Ribs
6 Ea. Cloves of Garlic
1 Bunch Thyme
1 Bottle Napa Valley Cabernet (750ml)
1 Cup Rémy Martin XO Excellence
4 Quarts Reduced Veal Stock
2 Ea. Shallots
1/2 lb. Shiitake Mushrooms
1/2 lb. Oyster Mushrooms
1/4 lb. Black Trumpet Mushrooms
1 lb. Spring Baby Leeks
1 Bunch Italian Parsley
6 Ea. Disks Of Truffle Polenta
1 Ea. Parsnips
(Fried for Garnish)

Rémy Poached Pineapple Tower

WITH CARAMELIZED BANANA AND VANILLA ICE CREAM. PAIRED WITH RÉMY 1738

METHOD

Combine ingredients for the syrup and bring to boil. Add medium diced pineapple; simmer for about 10 minutes until soft and cooked through. Drain pineapple in a china cap, reserve poaching liquid. Toss papaya with hot pineapple in a bowl. Spread out on a plastic lined sheet pan and chill; store in a deli's.

Sauce- Coconut Vanilla

In a saucepan, place milk, bean, rum and salt. Bring to boil and reduce to a simmer; simmer for 15 minutes or until reduced by 30%; whisk occasionally. Make a slurry with the starch and rum and whisk in. Return to a boil for 30 seconds.

Sauce- Raspberry

In a saucepan, place raspberries, bean, cider and salt. Bring to boil and reduce to a simmer; simmer for 15 minutes, whisk occasionally. Gently press berries in a chinois. You want to extract FLAVOR AND COLOR, NOT PULP. Place juice back on stove and return to a simmer; reduce by half. Make a slurry with the brandy and starch. Whisk in. Return to boil for 30 seconds. Strain again through a chinois and chill.

INGREDIENTS

3 Pineapple Each, Medium Dice
2 Each Papaya, Small Dice

For The Syrup:
1 Quart Pineapple Juice
1 Quart Apple Cider
1 Cup Sugar, Vanilla
5 Each Vanilla Beans, Recycled
Yield: 3 quarts

Sauce- Raspberry
8 Pieces Raspberries
1/4 Each Vanilla Bean, Split And Scraped
Pinch Salt
4 Cups Apple Cider
1 Tablespoon Cornstarch
1 Ounce Brandy
Yield: 1 quart

Chef Philippe Jeanty

BISTRO JEANTY

About the Chef...

Born in Champagne, France, **Philippe Jeanty's** family spent much of their time growing, raising and preparing food that essentially included vegetables, chickens, rabbits and lambs. Thus Philippe learned many of the basics of French home cooking.

At fourteen, his father helped him to get a kitchen position at *Moet & Chandon*, with Chef Joseph Thuet. Philippe came to California in 1977, to open the *Domaine Chandon Restaurant* in Yountville.

Twenty years of the highest awards established Jeanty as one of America's finest chefs. But with his heart and his family (wife and two daughters) in Yountville, he opened *Bistro Jeanty* in 1998. It was chosen as the *"Best New Restaurant in the Bay Area in 1998"* and chosen as one of four nominees for *"Best New Restaurant in America 1998"* by the James Beard Foundation.

About the Restaurant...

Picture this – a beret clad figure on a bicycle (pannier and all!) cheerfully whistling as he pedals along a narrow village road. He greets mid-morning strollers with a cheery wave, they wave back in recognition of Yountville's very own French chef. And one of its newest inhabitant. He arrives at his destination, a charming rustic old country cottage. The sign reads *"Bistro Jeanty"*. He rests the bicycle against the wall and enters...

Phillipe Jeanty is passion personified. His lifestyle, a certain measure of whimsical Gallic eccentricity and Bistro Jeanty – a charming hand-crafted restaurant, where his philosophy and flair for hearty paysan fare are so vividly illustrated, all make for a breath of fresh air, adding to the burgeoning restaurant center that is Yountville in the very heart of the Wine Country.

Stepping through the low doorway and waiting briefly for a much-in-demand table, you have to appreciate the rusticity of this bistro café, with its typical interior – all the hard work of Phillipe. With the aproned wait-staff, the oh-so French artifacts and posters, the great smell of cooking and the bustle, well it could be *a la campagne!*

he excels. As the word gets out, the lines seem to get longer. His offerings are meant to please, with such classics as Foie Blond (Duck pate with port poached pear) or another country favorite, Pieds de Cochon (pig's trotters) or Rillettes de Canard (Duck and Goat Cheese pate). As for the entrees, a more authentic Cassoulet (done the finite way with white baked beans, lashings of bacon, duck confit and sausage) you will not find.

And what better way to end this pleasant day trip to France than with a memorable Crepes Suzette served with orange butter and oodles of Cointreau.

Voila! Magnifique! Et merci, Monsieur le Chef!

Philippe Jeanty

Tournedos au Poivre

WITH CREAMY MUSHROOM CHARDONNAY SAUCE. PAIRED WITH RÉMY EXTRA

METHOD

Sauce Procedure:

Reduce shallots and wine over high heat until just dry. Add cream, mushrooms and thyme. Slowly simmer for 30 minutes. Season to taste. Strain through a fine strainer making sure to push down well on mushrooms to extract all the juice and flavors.

To serve:

Coat steaks well on both sides with pepper and season with salt. In a sauté pan with small amount of olive oil sear steaks well on both sides to form a crust. Roast in 400°f oven to desired doneness. Meanwhile, slowly cook shallots in 1 tbsp butter until tender. Add haricot verts, chicken stock and remaining butter, cook until stock has reduced and butter has thickened. Sauté sliced mushrooms in 2 tbsp of butter and 1 oz. olive oil. Season with salt and pepper. Add mushroom cream sauce. Reduce for about 5 minutes. Place haricot verts in bottom of bowl, place tournedos on top of green beans. Evenly spoon mushrooms over top of tournedos as well as 3-4 oz. of the cream sauce. Garnish with chopped Italian parsley.

INGREDIENTS

6 Each 8 oz.
Beef Tenderloin Steaks
1/2 Cup Large Cracked Black Pepper Sifted
1 lb Haricot Verts Or Regular Green Beans
– Blanched
1/2 Cup Shallots – Diced
1 Cup Chicken Stock
3-4 tbsp Butter
1 lb Button Mushrooms –
1/4 Sliced
Serves 6

For the sauce:
1/2 lb. shallots – sliced thin
12 oz. Chardonnay
1 1/2 lbs. Button mushrooms – sliced thin
1 quart cream
3 sprigs fresh thyme
Salt and pepper

Crepe Suzette

WARM CREPE WITH ORANGE BUTTER. PAIRED WITH RÉMY 1738

METHOD

For the Crepes:

Mix eggs and sugar. Warm half and half with vanilla bean and butter. Mix together all ingredients except milk. Add milk to consistency. Allow to rest for at least 1 hour.

For the butter:

With a top mixer or hand held, cream together sugar and butter until well mixed. Add Cointreau and orange zest, mix well. Refrigerate until ready to use.

To Serve: In a clean non-stick pan over high heat, heat pan well – until just smoking. Ladle in just enough batter to cover bottom of pan, you should hear a sizzling noise. The crepes cook very quickly, about 30 seconds per side. Gently pull crepe away from side of pan with a high heat spatula and turn over for 30 seconds longer. Keep slightly warm until ready to use or refrigerate. Spread a thin layer of the butter onto serving dish. Place crepe on top of butter, warm in oven for 2 minutes. Dust with powdered sugar and drizzle with Cointreau.

INGREDIENTS

For the Crepes:
(makes approx. 12-15 large crepes)
1½ Cups Cake Flour
½ Cup Sifted Powdered Sugar
¼ Cup Melted Clarified Butter
5 Eggs
1 Cup half and half
1 tbsp. Cointreau
16 oz. Whole Milk
1 Each Vanilla Bean –
Split & Scraped.

For the butter:
1lb Powdered Sugar
1lb Butter
½ Cup + 1 Tbsp Cointreau
2 Each Oranges – Outer Zest
Only – Chopped Well

Chefs Mitchell & Steven Rosenthal

POSTRIO

About the Chefs...

With a shared passion for cooking, **Mitchell** and **Steven Rosenthal** orchestrate all of the elements that comprise Postrio. Wolfgang Puck has given the Rosenthal brothers full reign at *Postrio*, and his San Francisco gem continues to shine. In the five years at *Postrio*, they have developed their own particular style of California cuisine. Mitchell says, " I work hard at taking the food and simplifying it... we concentrate the flavors in such a way that it just blows you away." Mitchell was originally anticipating a career in photojournalism with a Bachelor of Fine Arts from Manhattan's School of Visual Arts, when he brought home Paul Prudhomme's *"Louisiana Kitchen"* and cooked some of the recipes. He persistently called Paul Prudhomme weekly for six months before finally being accepted as an intern at *K. Paul's*. In 1989 he became one of the opening cooks for *Postrio*. He left *Postrio* after a year to further explore the culinary treasures of Asia and Europe. In 1994, Mitchell and Steven returned to San Francisco to become executive chefs at *Postrio*. Steven is passionate about perfecting technique, so he decided to expand his skills at the Culinary Institute of America, New York. After graduating in 1988 he went to work at the Pierre and then joined Mitchell as an opening cook at *Postrio*.

About the Restaurant...

Wolfgang Puck opened the tri-level restaurant, **Postrio**, on April 1, 1989, but upon entering this dramatic venue, you can see that the heart and soul of this restaurant lies in the hands of the brothers far from grim, Chefs Mitchell and Steven Rosenthal. Mr. and Sr., as their embroidered initials read on their aprons, have been entrusted by the Austrian Meister chef to faithfully convey his superlative brand of cooking. The result is an innovative menu, brilliantly presented by the two, reflecting an insightful foray into the Mediterranean and Asian cultures which are so prominent in San Francisco.

Before even looking at the menu I found myself surrounded by the striking décor of huge orbs, suspended from the ceiling, resembling an oceanic cluster of Goliathan clams, the vibrant art of Dale Chihuly and his "Persian series", conjuring up visions of sea creatures amidst swirls of rubies and tangerines. It's a truly unique décor that people seem to be talking about from California to New York (Chef David Burke of *Park Avenue Cafe* being one of the biggest fans.) But the gems on the menu outshine even the most stunning display of artwork on the walls and ceiling. Choices include Bacon Wrapped Wolfe Ranch Quail with manila clams, creamer potatoes and a garlic lemon glaze, or Creamy Truffle Polenta with shaved Prime Rib. Of course, I had already been indulged, by being seated, upon walking in (and without booking!) and then encouraged by the choice of starters. Tempting me were the Barron Point Oysters on the half shell with champagne Mignonette and cocktail sauce, or Stir fry Garlic Lamb with chili oil, ginger and fresh mint (sadly I had a meeting later with the editor!) But Postrio's "Fingal's Cave" theme influenced my decision to go 'Neptunian' with the Trio of Tuna with avocado, citrus ponzu, and truffle apple soy. Perfect!

To coin a well known phrase . . . *"Live, Love, Eat!"*

Mitchell Rosenthal
Steven Rosenthal

Caramel Apple Napoleon

WITH SUNDRIED CHERRY COMPOTE AND
BUTTERMILK ICE CREAM. PAIRED WITH RÉMY XO EXCELLENCE

INGREDIENTS

Makes 4 Napoleons
For The Caramel Apples and Sauce:
2 Cups Granulated Sugar
1 Cup Water
1 Tbsp. Light Corn Syrup
4 Tbsp. Unsalted Butter
2 Tsp. Calvados or Brandy
3 Large Granny Smith Apples, Peeled
1/2 Cup Apple Juice

For The Puff Pastry:
1 9"X12" Sheet Purchased Puff Pastry
1 Cup Water
1 Cup Granulated Sugar
2 Cinnamon Sticks

For The Sundried Cherry Compote:
1 Cup Soft Sundried Cherries
1/2 Cup Red Cooking Wine
6 Tbsp. Granulated Sugar
1 Cup Water
2 1/2 Tsp. Cornstarch
2 1/2 Tsp. Cold Water
1 Tbsp. Brandy or Kirsch

For The Buttermilk Ice Cream:
1 Cup Heavy Whipping Cream
5 Egg Yolks
1/2 Cup Granulated Sugar
1 Cup Buttermilk

METHOD

For the caramel apples and sauce: Preheat oven to 400°f. Spray a 9" x 12" metal baking pan with non-stick spray and set aside. Place each apple stem-side up on a cutting board. Slice downward, parallel to core, twice on each side of the core to make 4 circles per apple, each at least 1/4" thick, depending on the size of apple. Lay circles flat in a single layer in the baking pan. Once apples are ready, prepare the caramel: In a 4-quart saucepot, combine sugar, water and corn syrup. Bring to boil over medium-high heat, using a wet pastry brush to wash down any sugar crystals sticking to sides of the pot. Continue cooking until sugar begins to turn amber. Turn off heat and swirl pan to color evenly. Quickly whisk in butter and brandy and immediately pour caramel over apples, covering them entirely. Place apples in oven and cook until they are fork-tender and becoming translucent, about 15-20 minutes. Let apples cool 5 minutes, then transfer them to a plate with a fork or spatula. Add apple juice to baking pan and return to oven for a few minutes until juice starts to bubble. Whisk juice into caramel to deglaze the pan. Strain sauce into another container. Keep warm and adjust consistency with additional juice if necessary.

For the puff pastry: Thaw puff pastry according to package instructions. Cut out 12 x 3" circles and place on a flat parchment-lined baking sheet. Place circles in freezer until completely firm, at least 2 hours. Meanwhile, combine sugar, water and cinnamon sticks in a 2-quart saucepot. Bring to boil and simmer 2-3 minutes. Turn off heat and let steep for 30 minutes; discard cinnamon sticks. Preheat oven to 400°f. When puff circles are frozen, brush both sides with cinnamon stick syrup and return to baking sheet. Place another piece of parchment paper over circles and put another baking sheet filled with pie weights on top of them to keep the flat. Bake for 15 minutes, remove pan of weights and flip circles over. Place pan of weights back on top and continue cooking until circles are crisp and golden, 5-10 more minutes. Uncover and let cool.

For the sundried cherry compote: In a 2-quart saucepot, combine cherries, wine, sugar and 1 cup water. Bring to boil over medium-high heat, reduce and simmer 2-3 minutes. Turn off heat and let cherries steep for 15 minutes. In a small bowl, whisk together cornstarch and cold water. Whisk into cherries and return to boil, stirring constantly, for one minute. Add brandy off of heat. Set aside at room temperature until ready to serve.

For the buttermilk ice cream: Place egg yolks in medium bowl and set aside. Place 1-quart container or bowl inside another bowl filled with ice and set aside. Combine cream and sugar in small saucepot and bring just to a boil. Turn off heat. Quickly ladle some of hot cream into yolks, whisking the yolks constantly so that the hot cream does not curdle them. Continue ladling in cream until all of it has been added to the yolks. Strain mixture through fine mesh sieve into container on ice. Stir frequently until cool. Add buttermilk and freeze in ice cream maker according to manufacturer's directions. For best results, make ice cream at least 8 hours before assembling desserts.

To assemble the napoleons: Place baked puff pastry circles on a sheet pan lined with parchment and put an apple circle on top of each. When ready to serve, warm puff-apple circles in 350°f oven for about 10 minutes, until hot. Drizzle caramel sauce on plates, and stack three puff-apple circles on each plate. Use slotted spoon to place some cherries with out too much liquid onto each napoleon. Serve with a scoop of buttermilk ice cream on top or on the side of the napoleons.

Quail wrapped in Bacon

PAIRED WITH RÉMY 1738

METHOD

Stuff quails with herb mustard and wrap with raw bacon. Lightly pan sear them, then roast at 450°f for 7 minutes until medium rare. Brown potatoes in olive oil. After browned, wilt spinach with potatoes. Put olive oil in pan and heat. Add garlic and clams and cook just slightly. Add chicken demi and reduce by half. Add lemon juice, parsley, butter and chili flakes.

INGREDIENTS

Serves 4

8 Quails (Two per Person)	2 Tbsp. Garlic
4 Tbsp. Herb Mustard	2 Cups Chicken Demi
16 Slices Raw Bacon	3 Tbsp. Parsley
16 Creamer Potatoes	¼ lb. Butter
3 Cups Spinach	Chili Flakes To Taste
32 Manila Clams	

INGREDIENTS

Serves 4

16 oz. NY Steak Tartare, Chopped	1 Tbsp Dijon Mustard
Half Red Onion, Chopped	2 Tbsp. Indonesian Sweet Soy
2 Tbsp. Chopped Chives	2 Tbsp. Ketchup
¼ Cup Garlic Aioli	1 Tbsp. Tamarind
1 Tbsp. Fresh Wasabi	4 Quail Egg Yolks, Raw
	2 Radish, Julienned
	1 Bunch Watercress

Indonesian Steak Tartare

WITH RADISH AND WILD WATERCRESS.
PAIRED WITH RÉMY VSOP

METHOD

Mix the wasabi, aioli and mustard together. Separately, mix the ketchup, tamarind and Indonesian sweet soy. Then combine all ingredients except quail eggs, radish and watercress. Season with salt and pepper. Combine. Place a 2" metal ring in center of your serving plate. Pack the tartare inside and remove ring being careful to keep tartare in a circular shape. Make a small hole in center of the tartare and fill each one with a quail egg yolk. Garnish each plate with radish and watercress.

Chef Greg Atkinson

About the Chef...

Greg Atkinson creates the menu that defines *Canlis*. Reinventing classic dishes that made this the best place to dine in Seattle in 1950, Atkinson has made it all the more so in 2002. Partnering with a network of fishermen, farmers, and friends, Atkinson translates flavorful northwest ingredients into robust and refined dinners. A prolific writer, Atkinson is the author of "In Season" and "The Northwest Essentials Cookbook" *(Sasquatch Books, Seattle, 1997 and 1999.)* In 2000, Atkinson won the *M.F.K. Fisher Distinguished Writing Award* from the James Beard Foundation. As an authoritative voice on Northwest Cuisine, he is also in demand as one of the city's favorite cooking instructors.

With an emphasis on seasonal foods, simply prepared, Atkinson's meals reflect the rusticity of the Pacific Northwest, as well the sophistication of his earliest apprenticeships with Michelin-stars Roger Vergé and Regis Marcon in France.

About the Restaurant...

"Time present and Time past are both perhaps present in Time future, And Time future contained in Time past"

For more than 50 years, *Canlis*, a Seattle landmark, epitomizes almost to the letter these historic words by T S Eliot. Greg Atkinson and his wife of over 30 years, Alice, have faithfully preserved the timeless reputation of the late Peter Canlis' brainchild. Certainly, the continuing ascendancy of this classy establishment is not only the effect of the innovative *cuisine de terre* that provides such a definitive menu, but the wonderful energy that their marriage exudes. Atkinson has benefited magnificently from his apprenticeships in France under Grand Chefs Roger Verge and Regis Marcon and how it shows.

The sparkling romantic backdrop of Lake Union provides the essential stage for this gourmet's paradise and Chef Greg Atkinson's palate-entertaining food "show". Indeed, his menu is as much a visual impact, as (the man is a prolific wordsmith) it is literal. Many menus make simple statements, but Atkinson's descriptions always catch the eye. Peter Canlis' Prawns- pan sautéed with shrimp red chilies garlic and lime, and a Sonoma Foie Gras with a fantastic accompaniment of papaya port and vanilla bean, reach subliminal heights as preludes to this stellar performance. And who else would offer such unusual items such as a Bento Box of Vegetables described as a "Japanese frame for American farmers' seasonal works of art, asparagus, herbed fingerling potatoes and more". Most apt. Or the Wasyugyu Steak – an altogether different experience where he presents Kobe- style Washington beef, naturally raised from Japanese sires and Angus cows, with herb potatoes and his trademark, the organically grown market vegetables. And finally for the child within us, his "special" desserts. One that caught these eyes, the Rhubarb Crisp- home-grown crimson-red, rhubarb and candied ginger, ginger ice cream, is decidedly and wickedly indulgent.

Peter Canlis, wherever you may be, know that your passion continues. Greg and Alice, here's to another 50 years of excellence!

Greg Atkinson

Dungeness Crab Cake

WITH ORANGE BUTTER SAUCE
PAIRED WITH RÉMY XO EXCELLENCE

INGREDIENTS

**Serves 8 as appetizer
or 4 as an entrée**
1 Slice White Bread
1/4 Cup Milk
2 Cups Of Dungeness
Crab Meat (1 Pound)
1 1/2 Tablespoons Sweet Red
Pepper, Finely Chopped
1 1/2 Tablespoons Green Onions,
Finely Chopped
1 1/2 Tablespoons Sweet Pickle
Ginger, Finely Chopped
1/2 Cup Mayonnaise
1 Beaten Egg
Salt and Pepper to Taste
2 Cups Panko
4 Ounces Olive Oil
Orange Butter Sauce, Recipe
Follows
1 Cup Shredded Spinach
1/2 Cup Roasted Red Pepper
Purée, Recipe Follows
3 Tablespoons Orange Zest
8 Sprigs Italian Parsley

**Orange Butter Sauce
Yield: 10-12 oz**
1 1/2 Cups Fresh-Squeezed
Orange Juice
1/4 Cup Freshly Grated
Orange Zest
1 Teaspoon Kosher Salt
1 Cup (8 oz) Chilled Butter,
Cut Into 1-Inch Chunks

**Roasted Sweet Pepper Purée
Yield: about 1 cup**
2 Large Red Sweet Peppers
1 tbsp. Balsamic Vinegar
2 tbsp. Olive Oil

METHOD

Have all ingredients very cold. Cover bread with milk and set aside. In a mixing bowl, combine crabmeat, red pepper, green onions, and pickled ginger. Stir in mayonnaise and beaten egg. Squeeze milk from bread; discard excess milk and stir soaked bread into crabmeat mixture. Sprinkle half Panko onto a plate and set remaining Panko aside. Using a 4-ounce dish, press crab mixture into mounds and invert onto panko-covered plate. Press additional Panko onto each cake. Cakes may be prepared ahead up to this point and kept refrigerated for several hours or overnight.

Preheat oven to 425°f.

For each crab cake, pour 1/2 oz. oil into an ovenproof skillet, heat 1/2 oil over high heat. Refresh the Panko breading on the cake(s) to be cooked and sear on each side. Finish in oven for 5 minutes. Pour 1 oz. orange butter sauce on a hot plate and transfer sizzling hot crab cake onto pool of sauce. Garnish each serving with shredded spinach, a squirt of red pepper purée and a pinch of orange zest.

Orange Butter Sauce:

In a non-reactive saucepan over high heat, boil cider with salt and pepper until reduced to 1/2 cup. (Sauce base may be made ahead up to this point and kept refrigerated for several days.) Whisk butter into boiling reduced orange juice mixture to make smooth emulsified sauce. Sauce may be held in an insulated pitcher for several hours, or kept in very warm spot.

Roasted Sweet Pepper Purée:

Preheat oven to 425°f. Arrange peppers in single layer on a full sized sheet pan and bake 15 minutes, or until skin is blistered and blackened. Remove from oven. Transfer peppers to a brown paper bag and allow to stand, undisturbed 10-12 minutes, or until cool enough to handle. Peel peppers – skin should slip off easily. Rinse away any blackened bits, but avoid rinsing away flavorful juices. Remove stems. Gently split and seed each pepper. In a blender, purée roasted peppers with vinegar and olive oil.

Wasyugyu Tenderloin

WITH MARKET VEGETABLES. PAIRED WITH RÉMY VSOP

METHOD

Preheat grill and rub steaks with oil. In order to establish good grill marks, grill steak for 3-4 minutes in one position without disturbing then turn 45° and grill 3-4 minutes longer to make cross hatched marks on the same side. Turn steak and grill until steak reaches desired degree of doneness. Serve grilled steak on a hot plate with market vegetables.

Market Vegetables

Use the most colorful and flavorful vegetables you can find from your local farmers' market or green grocer. Put a quart of water and 2 tablespoons of kosher salt in a saucepan and cook the vegetables one type at a time in the boiling water.

INGREDIENTS

Serves 1
6-Ounce Tenderloin Steak
Vegetable Oil
Kosher Salt And Freshly
Ground Black Pepper
Market Vegetables, See Note

INGREDIENTS

Yield: four 8-oz. or eight 4-oz. cakes
8 Ounces Bittersweet Chocolate
½ Cup Butter
4 Medium Egg Yolks (¼ Cup)
2 Medium Egg Whites (¼ Cup)
¼ Teaspoon Salt

¼ Teaspoon Vinegar
3 Tablespoons Sugar
1 Cup Whipping Cream, Whipped With 2 Tablespoons Powdered Sugar
Mint Leaves, Strawberries, and Chocolate Fans For Garnish

Chocolate Lava Cake

PAIRED WITH RÉMY LOUIS XIII

METHOD

Butter 6 8-oz. soufflé dishes or 12 4-oz. disposable, aluminum baking cups. Arrange dishes on baking sheet and refrigerate. In a large stainless steel mixing bowl set over barely simmering water, melt chocolate and butter. In clean dry mixing bowl, whip egg whites with salt and vinegar until they hold soft peaks. Beat in sugar and continue whipping until whites are stiff. Set aside. Stir egg yolks into chocolate mixture and stir until smooth. Fold egg white mixture into chocolate mixture and transfer batter to a pastry bag fitted with a large metal tip. Pipe batter promptly into prepared, chilled dishes. Allow batter to chill for at least one hour. Preheat oven to 350°f and bake small cakes 8 minutes and large cakes 12 minutes, or until tops are crisp but insides are not set. Invert each warm cake onto a plate and garnish with a dollop of whipped cream, a strawberry, a mint leaf and a chocolate fan. Unbaked cakes may be kept refrigerated for three days, or frozen for three weeks.

Chef Kerry Sear

CASCADIA

About the Chef...

Kerry Sear imbues his passion for the Pacific Northwest to create *Cascadia's "Decidedly Northwest"* cuisine. Raised on a dairy farm in Warwickshire, England, Sear's childhood ambition was to become a graphic designer. After apprenticeship, at *Stratford-on-Avon de Vere Hotel*, Sear worked at several restaurants in England and Canada before being appointed to Executive chef at the *Four Seasons Hotel* in Vancouver. Sear earned international acclaim during his time there as well as in British Columbia, Toronto and recently in Seattle. He was personal chef to Queen Elizabeth II during the 1988 Commonwealth Conference in Vancouver, and for President Clinton during the 1993 APEC Leaders Dinner in Seattle. Awarded five gold medals at the 1987 World Culinary Olympics, Vancouver, and three others in the 1988 competition in Frankfurt, Sear has prepared dinner at the James Beard House, three times.

An accomplished artist, Sear hand sketches each dish prior to preparation. Globally recognized for his hand-painted decorative chef's jackets, Sear and his wife Heidi, formed their own company in 1993, *Chef, Art and Design*.

About the Restaurant...

What is it? Is it considered Northwestern or eclectic? Rather, the only way to describe Executive Chef, Kerry Sear's, Native American influenced cooking styles is *"Cascadian Cuisine."* Using the nearby mountain range as inspiration, Sear incorporates cedars, Douglas firs, and wild grasses for a variety of ways. But he doesn't just use them for decoration, he braises the branches into syrups to glaze dessert, and, just like the early Native Americans, uses grasses, hay and leaves to wrap poultry, meat and fish to keep in the juices, thus developing an aromatic flavor.

Since its opening in July of 1999, *Cascadia* has impressed guests with the presentation of its exquisite food. Vibrant, bold in flavor, color and texture, Chef Sear is truly an artist by nature, sketching the design of each dish prior to preparation.

Cascadia is the perfect blend of elegant fine dining and "ruggedness" of the Pacific Northwest. With a stunning view of Elliot Bay and the Olympic mountain range, Cascadia captures the natural beauty that Seattle has to offer in both cuisine and decor.

Savor the typical "Cascadia" freshness and flavor in such signature dishes as Oregon White Truffle, potato soup with juniper-berry toast, Warm Dungeness Crab on buttermilk herb pancake caviar, and pear wine sauce, or Wild Grass and Herb Baked Partridge with blackberry reduction. The Rosemary Basted Lamb Loin with grilled apples and straw-fries with a Pinot- noir glaze is also an excellent choice.

In addition to the a la carte menu, Cascadia offers four fixed menus entitled *"Wild & Gathered"*, *"The Season"*, *"From The Market"* and *"Decidedly Northwest".*

"North by Northwest" – indeed!

Stuffed Loin of Rabbit

ROASTED PEACH AND SWEET CORN WITH POMMES ANNA.
PAIRED WITH RÉMY 1738 OR XO EXCELLENCE

INGREDIENTS

Serves 4
For Rabbit:
4 lb. Saddle of Rabbit (De-Boned)
1 lb. Rabbit Kidneys and Trimmings
1 lb. Caul Fat
2 Tbsp Vegetable Oil
1 Branch Thyme
1 Cup Chopped Shallot
1 Cup Chopped Onion
1 Cup Brandy
2 Peaches
2 Ears Sweetcorn
1 Cup Blanched and Peeled Fava Beans
2 Cups Sugar

Pommes Anna
1½ lb Potatoes
2 oz. Clarified Butter
Salt, Pepper and Nutmeg to Taste

Sauce
3 Cups Rabbit Stock
1 Cup Peach Puree
1 oz. Sugar
1 Cup Red Wine Vinegar
1 Cup Brandy
1 Cup White Wine

METHOD

Place loin between 2 pieces of plastic wrap and pound flat to inch with butcher's mallet. Hold in refrigerator. Grind kidneys and trimmings in meat grinder. Add vegetable oil to frying pan and heat over high heat. Add shallot, onion and ground rabbit meat and sauté for 3 minutes. Add brandy and flambe. Season with salt and pepper. Cool. Lay out piece of caul fat approx. 8"x8". Place loin in center of fat. Place spoonful of ground rabbit mixture on loin and roll. Wrap roll with caul fat to hold in place. Season with salt and pepper. Hold in refrigerator. Pan sear stuffed rabbit loin over high heat to brown on each side. Finish in oven at 350°f for 20 minutes (or until meat in center reaches 155° for well done).

Vegetable and Peach Preparation:

While rabbit bakes, sate corn and fava beans until tender. Add salt and pepper to taste. Mix 2 cups sugar and 2 cups water. Boil until sugar dissolves. Simmer. Cut peaches in half and poach in syrup for 10 minutes. Peel peach halves. Set aside. (May be done ahead of time). Just before serving place peaches and sauce in baking dish and bake at 350°f until hot and slightly caramelized.

Sauce:

Bring sugar and red wine vinegar to boil. Lower heat to medium. Cook until thickened to syrup consistency. Add brandy and white wine. Reduce by half. Add peach puree and rabbit stock. Continue to cook until sauce reaches syrup consistency.

Pommes Anna:

Slice raw potatoes to ⅛" thickness. Season with salt, pepper and a pinch of nutmeg. In a sauté pan heat clarified butter over high heat. Layer potato slices to cover bottom of pan. Continue to layer evenly until 1" thick. Lower heat to medium and cook until golden brown. Flip potatoes and place in 350°f oven for 10 minutes.

To Serve:

Place pommes Anna in center of plate. Spoon corn and fava beans around pommes Anna. Slice rabbit loin in wheel and place over pommes Anne. Place peach half on top and spoon sauce over corn and fava beans.

Mushroom Stuffed Mushrooms

METHOD

Set aside 2 Portobello mushrooms, 8 Morel mushrooms, and 8 Crimini mushrooms. These will be used for filling later. Heat saucepan over medium heat. Add ½ butter to melt. Add onions and stir until soft (do not brown). Add remaining mushrooms. Stir well. Add wine and season with salt and pepper. Cook until mushrooms are soft. Add two tsp of herbs. Allow to cool. Chop mixture. This can be done by hand or in a food processor. Be careful not to purée too much. Chill in refrigerator. Using chopped mixture, fill cavities of saved mushrooms (for Portobellos, dark side on top) Place onto a buttered sheet pan.

Mix together remaining herbs with breadcrumbs and sprinkle onto each stuffed mushroom. This will help soak any moisture and create a crust. Place into a pre-heated oven at 375°f. Bake for 5 minutes. Sauté sliced lobster mushrooms in butter. Season with salt and pepper, over medium heat. Cook until soft, these mushrooms will remain crisp even when cooked. Lay these on plate as a garnish, and place stuffed mushrooms on top. Serve with a reduction of port wine and mountain black huckleberries, garnish with parsley and chives.

INGREDIENTS

Serves 4
Huckleberry Reduction:
3 Pack Small Portobello Mushrooms with Stem Removed (Peeled and Lightly Sautéed)
16 Pack Large Morel Mushrooms with Stem Removed
1lb Crimini Mushrooms (Caps Only)
8 oz. Lobster Mushrooms (Washed and Thinly Sliced)
4 oz. White Button Mushrooms (Chopped)
3 oz. Onions, Peeled And Diced
2 oz. White Wine
3 Tsp Parsley and Thyme, Chopped
4 Tsp Breadcrumbs
4 oz. Butter
Salt and Pepper
½ Cup Chopped Chives and Parsley for Garnish

Chef Francesco Ricchi

ETRUSCO

About the Chef...

In the Tuscan hills sits the centuries-old village of Cercina, home of the Ricchi family. *Francesco Ricchi's* grandfather opened a small grocery store and trattoria. Many years later, young *"Cesco,"* with his parents, turned this into a successful restaurant that still attracts the accolades. Continuing the tradition of serving the finest quality food at affordable prices, Chef Ricchi opened *Cesco Trattoria,* and *Etrusco Trattoria* in the nation's capital city.

Francesco has earned his establishments dozens of awards, including such honors as *Best New Restaurant* in the United States *(Esquire magazine);* Distinguished Restaurant of North America Award; Top Twenty-Five Restaurants in North America *(Food & Wine);* Restaurant Hall of Fame (American Restaurant Association).

He is highly regarded by his peers and industry professionals for his contribution to the food industry, his culinary skills, as well as his humanitarian efforts. He was voted the *1998 Chef of the Year* by the Restaurant Association of Metropolitan Washington.

About the Restaurant...

Chef Francesco Ricchi brings warmth and family tradition to DC, with *Etrusco* in the heart of the capital and *Cesco Trattoria,* just minutes away from downtown Washington. The interior is typically Tuscan with golden stone colored arched walls, rustic brown and red brick pillars and a soft glowing light.

The Florentine native got his start in the culinary business in Cercina, Italy, when his grandfather opened a small grocery store and trattoria catering to the locals. These days, Chef Ricchi, affectionately called "Cesco," attracts people looking for authentic Italian, from all over, to his twin sister restaurants Cesco and Etrusco.

An absolute must is the Insalata Di Indivia Al Parmigiano Croccante, (deliciously light endive and balsamic salad, presented in a dramatically tall manner, in a shell of crispy baked parmesan cheese). Typical of Tuscan food, the flavor and ingredients are honest and straightforward but the display is magnificent. The Sautéed Venison Loin, served with dried fruit sauce, string beans and wild mushrooms, or Linguine with Shrimp, squid, scallops, clams and mussels, are both entrees that will take you back to your first trip to Italy.

With two successful restaurants underway, television appearances on the Discovery Channel's *"Great Chefs of the East,"* and numerous awards, Chef Ricchi has clearly grasped the right blend of good food, ambiance and romance that is sure to spark a love affair with the flavor of Tuscany, captured intrinsically, in his cuisine. No matter how much you may protest to dessert, after the rather large and certainly filling portions, the dining experience would not be complete without sharing a wedge of the typical Florentine cake, Zuccatta. It's a chocolate mousse dome, flavored with rum, peach schnapps, and served with whipped cream and raspberry sauce – certainly worthy of indulgence!

Zuccatto

Zuccatto

PAIRED WITH RÉMY 1738

METHOD

Sponge cake procedure:

Put egg yolks and sugar in bowl and whip well. Whip egg whites until stiff. Combine with egg yolk mixture and incorporate flour and vanilla carefully. Coat a sheet pan with butter and flour and pour the mixture into the sheet pan. Bake for 30-40 minutes at 300°f.

Succoth procedure:

Mix heavy cream with granulated and powdered sugar. Use half the mixture and whip to right consistency. Add bittersweet chocolate chips. Mix other half with cocoa powder and whip to right consistency. Mix in crushed hazelnuts. Cut an 8-inch round from sponge cake and the rest into triangles that can fit from the center of the mold to the outside. Brush liquor mixture onto sponge cake laid into mold. Add white whipped cream mixture into bottom of the mold and up the sides. Fill center with chocolate whipped cream mixture. Cover with the round sponge cake layer and brush with remainder of liquor mixture. Wrap in plastic wrap and refrigerate for 3-4 hours.

To serve, unmold and sprinkle with powdered chocolate and powdered sugar and cut into wedges.

INGREDIENTS

1 Quart Heavy Cream
3 oz. Ounces Hazelnuts, Toasted And Crushed
4 oz. Bittersweet Chocolate Chips
3 oz. Granulated Sugar
3 oz. Powdered Sugar
$2/3$ Cup Rums And $1/3$ Cup Peach Schnapps
4 oz. Cocoa Powder

Sponge cake (pan di spagna)
4 Eggs
6 oz. Sugar
5 oz. Cake Flour
1 Teaspoon Vanilla
8 Inch Round Mold
(Plastic or Stainless Steel)
Half Sheet Pan

Pappardelle All'Anatra

M E T H O D

Sauce: Heat olive oil with duck cut into pieces. Add salt, pepper, crushed garlic, thyme and basil. Brown duck and add to the pan onion, carrot, celery, parsley and gently sauté. Cook until liquid from the vegetables is evaporated. Pour in wine and reduce. Add tomatoes and tomato paste. Check for salt and pepper. Cook over a low heat for one hour or until duck meat is removable. Add water if needed. Remove duck from the sauce, de-bone and cut meat in pieces. Finish cooking adding hot water or boiling stock for one hour or so.

Pasta: Sift flour on a pastry board and make a well in the center. Break eggs into well. Add salt and a spoon of olive oil. Mix eggs into flour and work dough energetically with your hands for 7-8 minutes. Leave it to rest for 30 minutes covered with a bowl or plastic wrap. Roll dough through a pasta machine to the desired thickness. Sprinkle with flour to prevent sticking. Cut sheet of pasta to one inch wide with a wheel. In a pot of abundant boiling salted water, add fresh pasta and cook for 30 seconds. Strain pasta and sauté with sauce in sauté pan adding Parmesan cheese as desired. Sprinkle with fresh parsley and serve.

INGREDIENTS

8 Large Fresh Squid	Rosemary, Finely Chopped
12 Shrimp (U20)	
2 Sweet Onions	Garlic, Finely Chopped
4 Plum Tomatoes	Mixed Greens
8 Wooden Skewers	Lemon Juice
Thyme, Finely Chopped	Extra Virgin Olive Oil

INGREDIENTS

3 - 4 lbs. Duck (With Liver and Heart)	1 lb. Italian Canned Tomatoes
1 Large Onion Chopped Coarsely	1 Tbsp. Tomato Paste
1 Large Carrot Chopped Coarsely	1/2 Cup Olive Oil
1-2 Stalks Celery Chopped Coarsely	Pinch Fresh Thyme
	Pinch Fresh Basil
2 Tbsp. Italian Parsley, Chopped	Pinch Pepper Flakes
	Salt and Pepper
5 Cloves Garlic	**Pasta**
8 oz. Red Wine	2 Lbs. All Purpose Flour
1 lb. Fresh Plum Tomatoes, Very Ripe, Chopped	7-8 Eggs
	7-9 Salt
	7-10 Olive Oil

Grilled Calamari

M E T H O D

Wash and clean fresh squid. Cut in 3/4 inch rings. Wash and remove shell of shrimp. Cut onion into wedges the same size as shrimp and squid. Cut tomato into quarters. Using double skewers, start with onion, shrimp, tomato, and squid. Repeat three times. Season with salt and pepper and fresh herbs. Sprinkle with olive oil and grill each side. Carefully remove the skewers and place on plate with mixed greens as a garnish. Sprinkle with emulsion of lemon juice and olive oil.

Chef Doug Anderson

SEASONS AT THE FOUR SEASONS

About the Chef...

Doug Anderson developed his appreciation for this country's rich variety of cooking styles while traveling with, and serving as a cook for the U.S. Coast Guard. This experience led to a love of the sea, and a fondness for exploration – both geographical and culinary.

Anderson's signature style is inspired by Eastern Shore regional cuisine. In the last twenty years, he has become proficient in the cooking styles of Boston, Chicago, San Francisco and Vancouver.

Seeking exposure to the Pacific Northwest, he accepted the position of Executive Chef of *Four Seasons Vancouver* in April 1998, where he received a Lifetime Achievement Award from *Vancouver* Magazine.

Since then, he has been meeting with local farmers to discover first-hand the wealth of produce available. His seasonal menus showcase his unique North American style and artful handling of seasonal ingredients.

About the restaurant...

"I guess it just proves that in America anyone can be President." President Gerald Ford. But if this dream is never realized in our lifetimes then we can certainly feel like a president at the *Seasons Restaurant* in Washington D.C. where an attentive wait staff and talented line of chefs give each and every guest the royal treatment. The pampering begins when Carlos Landazuri, Maitre D' of Seasons for the past 22 years, greets his guests. His kind nature, coupled with his expert professionalism, sets the standard for an elegant dining experience in this spacious yet romantic location, where the tables are set with a simple red rose.

In the kitchen, Executive Chef Doug Anderson, who recently took over from longtime Chef Doug McNeill, prepares exquisite menus that showcase his unique North American style and masterful handling of seasonal ingredients of the region. Examples are the flavorful Curry Battered Soft Shell Crab in a plum stew with toasted coconut for a first course, and the Orange and Ginger Glazed Duck Breast and Leg with hand rolled semolina gnocchi and "well cooked" savoy cabbage. Each dish demonstrates Chef Anderson's artful blend of flavors and shows that his experience at the Four Seasons Chicago and Vancouver are paying off at this flagship location. This magnificent city exudes a certain sense of power, pride and importance but it also maintains a quiet and subdued charm in the historic streets of Georgetown, which is reflected perfectly in Seasons Restaurant. As a final patriotic gesture, try the light and seemingly sinless Pinnacle of Passion Fruit dessert – a tart passion fruit sorbet enclosed in a White House-shaped meringue.

Doug Anderson

Lobster with Tamarind Glaze

PAIRED WITH RÉMY VSOP

INGREDIENTS

4 pcs - 2 lbs. Lobsters-
Boiled In A Large Amount
Of Water For 7 Minutes.
Chilled and Shelled.
1½ lbs. Baby Bok Choy -
Washed And Quartered
1 Cup Rice Vinegar
½ Cup Sugar
½ Cup Water
2 Bay Leaves
1 Tablespoons Crushed
White Pepper
3 Star Anis
1 Pack Rice Noodles
¼ Cup Sliced Green Onion
2 Tablespoons Sesame Oil
½ Cup Tamarind Paste
1 Tsp. Chili Oil
4 Roasted Garlic Cloves
1 Tsp. Dried Mustard Seeds,
Toasted And Ground
1 Tablespoons Brown Sugar
2 Cups Strained Orange Juice
1 Sliced Shallot
¼ Cup White Wine
1 Cup Grape Seed oil

METHOD

Tamarind Sauce:
Blend- Roasted Garlic, Tamarind Paste, Chili Oil, Mustard Seeds, Brown Sugar, 1 Cup water.

Pickled Bok Choy:
In a pot, combine sugar, vinegar, crushed white pepper, Anis, bay leaves, water. Bring to a boil. In a shallow pan, lay out bok choy. Pour boiling mixture over and let steep overnight.

Rice Noodles:
Blanch dried noodles in large amount of water for 2 minutes. Strain and cool. Toss noodles with sesame, scallions, season with salt and pepper. Spread noodles, in small rounds, on griddle top and toast brown on both sides.

Orange Essence:
Combine orange juice, shallot, white wine, bay leaves, in small saucepan. Reduce by ¾. Cool and place mixture in blender. Slowly add Grape seed oil, season with salt and pepper.

Assembly:
Sauté shelled Lobster in a pan with tamarind for five minutes until blanched lobster is fully cooked. The Tamarind should be slightly caramelized on the Lobster. Warm pickled bok choy; add some steamed carrots. Place on toasted rice cake and drizzle with Orange essence.

Dry Aged 12 oz. New York Steak

VERMONT CHEDDAR-CARAMELIZED ONION "TATER
TOT", BUTTERED ASPARAGUS, MUSHROOM SAUCE.
PAIRED WITH RÉMY XO EXCELLENCE OR VSOP

M E T H O D

Season Steak with Kosher Salt and Freshly ground black pepper. Brush with grape seed oil and grill to perfection, let rest.
Tater Tot: In a heavy pan, caramelize diced onion with 1 tbsp butter, 1 tbsp olive oil, salt and pepper. Steam diced potatoes for ten minutes (translucent but still firm).

In a bowl combine warm diced potatoes, Vermont Cheddar, caramelized onions, potato flour, salt and pepper to taste. Press mixture in a cone mold and fry until golden brown.
Sauce: Sauté assorted cleaned mushrooms, deglaze with Rémy Martin VSOP. Add white wine, veal glace, thyme and Rosemary. Reduce by half; add heavy cream, finish by whisking in 1 tbsp whole butter. Pass and hold. This dish is served with steamed jumbo asparagus and crisp large onion ring.

I N G R E D I E N T S

Serves 4
12 oz. Dry Aged Black
Angus NY Strip Steaks
20 Pieces Jumbo Asparagus
1 lb. Assorted Seasonal
Mushrooms
3 Thinly Sliced Shallots
2 Tbsp. Chopped Thyme
and Rosemary

Tater Tot:
4 Small Diced Russet
Potatoes
1/2 Cup Aged Vermont
Cheddar Cheese, Grated
1 Small Diced Sweet Onion
(Vadalia or Walla Walla)
1/4 Cup Potato Flour

I N G R E D I E N T S

4 Large Scoops
Passion Fruit Sorbet
4 Small Scoops
Vanilla Ice Cream
2 Egg Whites

4 oz. Granulated Sugar
1/8 Sheet Of Sponge Cake
Passion Fruit Puree
4 Crystallized Pansies

Passion Fruit Pinnacle

PAIRED WITH RÉMY VSOP

M E T H O D

Scoop passion sorbet into a large pyramid-shaped (or any other shape) flexi pan. Freeze. With a scoop, create a hollow from bottom of pyramid (while still in flexi pan.) Fill in the hollowed-out section with vanilla ice cream. Freeze. Heat egg whites and sugar over a water bath. When sugar is dissolved, whip in mixer on high speed until cool. Cut out sponge cake to the size of pyramid bottom. Unmold pinnacle onto the cake. Pipe meringue onto pinnacle, following the lines of the pyramid.
To serve:

Torch meringue to golden color and place on plate. Drizzle with passion fruit puree and garnish with crystallized pansy.

Chef Ris La Coste

1 7 8 9

About the Chef...

Graduating from Berkeley in French and biology, **Ris La Coste's** postgraduate studies in Paris helped her to meet Anne Willian at *La Varenne* Cooking School, where she earned her grand diplôme.

After a stint in *Burgundy*, Lacoste returned in 1982 joining Bob Kinkead at the *Harvest* in Cambridge, Massachusetts and then *21 Federal* in Nantucket in 1985, with *Washingtonian* magazine naming them *"Restaurateurs of the Year."*(1992)

In 1995 Ris took on *1789*, earning superb recognition, including: *"Chef of the Year"* in 1999, *"Restaurant of the Year"* in 2000 (The Capital Restaurant & Hospitality Awards program) and a continuing DiRoNA award, in 2001.

In 1999 Ris was nominated for the James Beard Foundation *"Best Chef: Mid-Atlantic Region"* and was guest chef at the notable Greenbrier Resorts' *La Varenne*.

Lacoste also fund-raises for Taste of the Nation, American Farmland Trust, Zoofari, Share Our Strength, D.C. Rape Crisis Center, Arena Stage, St. Jude Hospital for Children, and Food and Friends in Washington.

About the Restaurant...

Walking into Ris Lacoste's *1789* Restaurant feel likes coming home. Set in a gas-lit 19th Century Federal townhouse, just off the uneven pavement of Prospect Street, this historic restaurant makes you want to take a table by the fireplace and kick off your shoes – of course, jackets are required, but they didn't say anything about shoes!

Guests feel welcome and comfortable amongst the eclectic assortment of antiques that decorate the main dining rooms – there are five in total including the pub – although the work in the kitchen is anything but laid back. Chef Lacoste, named *"Chef of the Year"* in 1999, and nominated as *"Best chef: Mid Atlantic Region"* for the James Beard Foundation, lives up to high expectations. Educated in French and Biology at University of California at Berkeley and at *La Verenne* Cooking School in France, she creates hearty seasonal American cuisine that is both classic and original. Her Shrimp and Grits, for example is a perfect start to a 1789 dinner, served with fried green tomatoes and Smithfield ham. And her famous Roasted Rack of American Lamb served with Merlot sauce and delicious creamy fetta potatoes, makes guests come back year after year after year, gaining the same kind of trust we have with our mothers' cooking.

For those looking to complete a traditional evening of dinner and the theatre, Ris also offers a Pre-theatre menu. The Poached Alaska Salmon or Pine Nut Crusted Chicken as the entree, and either Crème Brûlée or Valrhona Chocolate Raspberry Torte for dessert, help to keep the decision-making to a minimum, in time for curtain up.

Grilled Lobster

WITH PEA SHOOTS AND GINGER LIME SAUCE.
PAIRED WITH RÉMY VSOP

INGREDIENTS

6 1½ lb. Lobsters
2 Cups Beurre Blanc Made
With ½ Cup White Wine, ½
Cup Tarragon Or White Wine
Vinegar, 2 Sliced Shallots, 1 lb.
Butter, Salt and Ground
White Pepper.
½ Cup Ginger Lime
Glaze – See Recipe
1 Bottle Inner Beauty Hot
Sauce – Or Other Jamaican
Habanero Chili Type
Condiment
Soy Molasses Glaze Made
From 6 oz. Soy Sauce, 3 oz.
Molasses, 1 oz. Red Wine
Vinegar
6 Cups Fresh Pea Shoots
1 Red Pepper, Cut Into
Julienne
3 Scallions, Cut Into 1" Batons
1 lb. Sugar Snap Peas, Blanched
2 Mango, Cut into Wide
Julienne
1 Lime, Cut Into 6 Wedges
2 Tablespoons Peanut Oil
Ginger Beurre Blanc
8 Shallots, Sliced
4 Sprigs Fresh Tarragon,
Coarsely Chopped
(Stems OK)
1 Bulb Ginger, Thinly Sliced
(Skin OK)
1 Cup White Wine
½ Cup Tarragon Vinegar
½ Cup Heavy Cream
1½ lb. Cold Butter,
Cut Into Cubes
3-4 oz. Lime Juice
3-4 oz. Ginger Glaze
Salt and White Pepper
Ginger Glaze
8 Bulbs Ginger, Peeled and
cut Into Very Fine Threads
Zest Of 8 Limes
3 Cups Tarragon Vinegar
1½ Cups Sugar
Soy Molasses Glaze
1 Quart Molasses
2 Quarts Soy Sauce
Dash Of Red Wine Vinegar

METHOD

Make the ginger lime glaze days in advance.

Make the beurre blanc no more than 1 hour before serving.

Add ½ cup of the ginger lime glaze (or to taste) to the beurre blanc and keep in a warm BUT NOT HOT place.

To prepare the lobsters: Remove claws and tails from bodies. Discard bodies or freeze and save for future lobster stock. Bring a large pot of water to boil. Prepare an ice bath to shock lobsters once they are cooked. To partially cook lobsters, add claws first to boiling water and let cook 2 minutes. Add tails and cook 3 minutes longer. (Claws take a bit longer to cook.) Remove from boiling water and place into ice bath to stop cooking process. Remove from cold water as soon as they are chilled. Crack claws and knuckles and remove meat as in tact as possible. Cut through under side of tails in half lengthwise. Keep covered in refrigerator until ready to use. Lobsters can be cooked earlier in the day for easier service.

To serve: Heat grill. Brush lobster lightly with Inner Beauty Hot Sauce and generously with molasses glaze. Grill lobster very briefly, a couple of minutes on each side for tails and just a minute or so for claws and knuckle meat. If grill spaces are too large for knuckle meat, place on foil and poke a few holes to allow the smoky flavor to penetrate the meat. Alternatively, roast everything. Remove to a platter until ready to plate.

Heat peanut oil in large sauté pan or wok until almost smoking. Cooking very quickly, as in a stir-fry, add red peppers, scallions, snap peas and pea shoots. Add a bit of soy molasses glaze and Inner Beauty. Cook, tossing constantly, until pea shoots have just wilted. Add mango and toss once more. Taste for seasoning and adjust. Place a portion of vegetable mix in center of each plate. Surround with flavored beurre blanc. Moisten lobster with a bit of beurre blanc and place two lobster tail halves on top of vegetables. Arrange claws and knuckle meat around the plate. Garnish with wedge of lime and encourage your guests to use just a squeeze on the lobster.

Ginger Beurre Blanc: In a stainless steel pot, reduce first five ingredients to dry. Add heavy cream and reduce to tacky. Mount with cold butter, whisking in a few cubes at a time on and off heat. Strain through a fine mesh. Add lime juice, ginger glaze and salt and white pepper.

Ginger Glaze: In a stainless steel pot, bring all ingredients to a boil. Remove from heat and let infuse, for 5 minutes. Return to heat and bring to a boil. Remove from heat and let infuse, for 5 minutes. Return to heat for a third time and bring to boil. Remove from heat.

Soy Molasses Glaze: Combine all ingredients

Rack of Lamb

PAIRED WITH RÉMY XO EXCELLENCE

METHOD

Melt 2 oz. of the butter in a sauté pan. Add diced onion and cook until soft but not browned. Add minced garlic and cook one minute longer. Remove cooked onions and garlic to a bowl and set aside to cool. When the mixture has reached room temperature add crumbled feta and mix well. This mixture can be made up to 3 days in advance and kept covered in the refrigerator.

To make the gratin, set oven at 350°f. To avoid discoloration, slice potatoes one at a time, as you need them, to create each layer. Remove a potato from water and slice it on mandoline in ⅛" thick slices and line the bottom of an 8"x6"x2" baking dish or any similar available dish. Season layer with pepper. Do not salt, as the feta is salty enough. Add another layer of potatoes and season again with pepper. Cover with a layer of onion/feta mix. Pour over heavy cream just barely to the level of potato. Press down each layer as you create them – potatoes should be just sitting in the cream and not completely covered by it. Repeat process two more times, then top with double layer of potato resulting in 8 layers of potato and 3 layers of onion/feta mix. When done, press down and make sure potatoes are just barely sitting in the cream. The potatoes will give off water as they cook so it is important not to add too much liquid. Cover with foil and cook until cream is bubbling and, more importantly, until potatoes in center of dish are fork tender, at least 1 hour. It is better to slightly overcook than undercook potatoes. Remove from oven, top with thin coating of breadcrumbs. Return to oven uncovered and cook until crumbs are golden. Remove from oven, recover with the foil and set aside in a warm place for the cream to set and thicken for at least 20 minutes. If cut into immediately, the cream would be too runny.

Heat olive oil in heavy-based pan. Add onion, carrot, celery and bell peppers and cook until all soft, stirring occasionally. Puree for at least 2 minutes in blender with 2-3 oz. stock and harissa. Season with salt and pepper. Roast lamb scraps until well browned. Meanwhile, in large saucepot, heat oil and add onions, carrot and celery. Cook until vegetables are lightly browned. Add roasted lamb and deglaze roasting pan with Merlot. Add Merlot and juices from pan. Add veal or lamb stock and bouquet garni, bring to boil and simmer until reduced by ⅓ or until desired sauce consistency is reached. Skim often to remove unwanted fat and impurities. Add about ½ cup red pepper puree and strain all through a fine mesh chinois. Season with salt and pepper to taste. If adding more red pepper puree, make sure to repass sauce through chinois. Keep warm until ready to use. Sauce can be made a day ahead and reheated.

To put together lamb dish: Set the oven to 450°f. Rub each lamb rack with lamb marinade and season well with salt. Set lamb on a roasting sheet and cook for 8 minutes. Remove from oven and let sit for 20 minutes. Just before serving return to the oven and cook for 3-5 minutes longer for medium rare. It is hard to judge how long to cook the rack since ovens are different and rack size varies. Second cooking may vary in time depending on desired doneness and the rack should rest a moment again before serving.

Sauté spinach in butter with a little water and salt. Heat sauce. Cut potatoes into 6 equal portions. Place a portion of potato at 2 o'clock and a pile of spinach at 10 o'clock. Cut each rack into 4 double chops and place two chops on each plate, bones crossing at noon. Ladle about 2 oz. of sauce onto plate and serve.

INGREDIENTS

3 - 8-Chop, Large Eyed Racks Of Domestic Lamb, Trimmed To The Loin, Bones Fully
Exposed and Scraped
1 Cup Lamb Marinade
Salt
6 Cups Spinach, Well Cleaned
2 oz. Butter
2 Cups Lamb Sauce
Creamy Feta Potatoes
Serves 6
Lamb marinade
¼ Cup Chopped Fresh Parsley
¼ Cup Fresh Cracked Black Pepper
¼ Cup Garlic, Minced
Zest Of 2 Lemons, Finely Chopped
1 Cup Olive Oil
Yields: 1½ cups
Combine all ingredients. Make marinade up to 2 weeks ahead and keep covered in the refrigerator.
Creamy Feta Potatoes
2 oz. Butter
1 Large Onion, Finely Diced
2 Cloves Garlic, Minced
10 Ounces Imported Greek Feta Cheese, Crumbled
6 Large Idaho Potatoes, Peeled and Covered with Water to Prevent Discoloration
Fresh Cracked Black Pepper
2 Cups Heavy Cream
⅔ Cup Bread Crumbs
Serves 6-8
Lamb Merlot Sauce
1" Lamb Scraps/Stew Meat with As Little Fat as Possible
2 oz. Olive Oil
1 Onion, Coarsely Chopped
1 Carrot, Coarsely Chopped
1 Stalk Celery, Coarsely Chopped
1 Cup Merlot
6 Cups Veal Stock Or Lamb Stock, If Available
1 Bouquet Garni of Rosemary, Thyme and Bay Leaf
½ Cup Red Pepper Puree
Salt And Fresh Cracked Black Pepper
Red Pepper Puree
2 oz. Olive Oil
1 Small Onion, Coarsely Chopped
1 Carrot, Coarsely Chopped
1 Stalk Celery, Coarsely Chopped
2 Red Bell Peppers, Stem and Seeds Removed, Coarsely Chopped
2-3 oz. Veal or Lamb Stock
1 Tbsp. Harissa

Personal Pairing Notes

(Match your favourite restaurant dish with the appropriate Rémy Cognac)

Restaurant	Dish	Cognac

The Spirit of Excellence

Restaurant	Dish	Cognac

The Spirit of Excellence

Mementos